BUILD YOUR OWN
acoustic guitar

BUILD YOUR OWN
acoustic guitar

▶ Complete instructions and full-size plans

Jonathan Kinkead

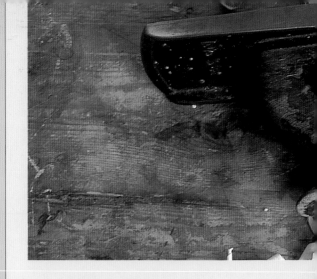

A QUARTO BOOK

Published by
Hal Leonard Corporation
7777 West Bluemound Rd
P.O. Box 13819
Milwaukee, WI 53213 USA

Trade Book Division Editorial Offices:
151 West 46th Street, 8th Floor
New York, NY 10036

Visit Hal Leonard online at
www.halleonard.com

International Standard Book No.:
0-634-05463-5

Library of Congress Control Number:
2003110370

First Edition

10 9 8 7 6 5 4 3 2 1

QUAR.BYOG

Conceived, designed, and produced by
Quarto Publishing plc
The Old Brewery
6 Blundell Street
London N7 9BH

Editor: *Kate Tuckett*
Art Editors: *Karla Jennings, Jill Mumford*
Assistant Art Director: *Penny Cobb*
Copy editor: *Claire Waite Brown*
Proofreader: *Anne Plume*
Designer: *Karin Skånberg*
Illustrator: *Kuo Kang Chen*
Photographer: *Pat Athie*
Indexer: *Pamela Ellis*

Art director *Moira Clinch*
Publisher *Piers Spence*

Manufactured by *Universal Graphics Pte Ltd*
Singapore

Printed by *Midas Printing International Ltd*
Hong Kong

▶ contents

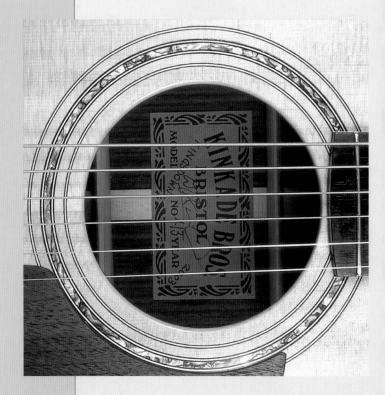

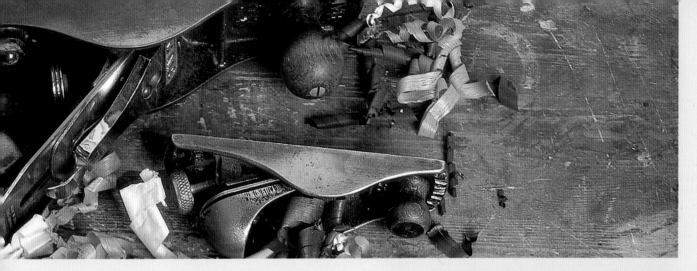

Introduction

- **The making of a luthier**
- **The Kinkade guitar**
- **Body shapes and sizes**
- **The power of the uncarved block**
- **Guitar making as therapy**

◄ *C.F. Martin's "O.M." guitar was designed in 1929 and provided the inspiration for many others—including the one featured in this book.*

THE MAKING OF A LUTHIER

My love affair with the guitar began in the 1960s, not long after my first encounter with the music of The Beatles and their contemporaries. I bought my first instrument, a cheap, steel-string acoustic, at the age of ten and learnt the rudiments of playing from my art teacher during the school lunchbreak. In time, other guitars arrived in our household; my brother Simon shared my interest and introduced me to folk and blues. I was a keen builder of model boats and aeroplanes and these practical skills stood me in good stead as I learnt to repair and adjust our guitars, and those of friends, to their optimum playability and potential.

At sixteen I built my first instrument: I fancied learning the bass but I couldn't afford to buy one, much less an amplifier. So I designed and built an acoustic bass guitar. It had a coffin-shaped plywood body—I had no idea how to create a curve—with sides formed from a series of flat panels. The neck was carved from a piece of oak salvaged from my bedposts, and the fretboard was fashioned from ¼ in (6mm) plywood. The soundhole was a double paisley shape, a fashionable pattern at the time. I purchased tuning machines and fret wire, and persuaded a friend to braze together a brass tailpiece of my own design.

The instrument was played held between the legs, like a cello. In retrospect, what was surprising was not that it worked, but that it worked so well. This was the start of my journey as a luthier. Now three decades and some 400 guitars later, I feel very fortunate to have been able to devote my life to my passion and earn a living from it.

THE KINKADE GUITAR

The acoustic steel-string flat-top guitar whose construction is described in this book is derived from a popular design by C.F. Martin, perhaps the greatest of American guitar makers. It was first built, so the story goes, in response to a request from an eminent banjo player for a guitar that felt like a banjo, and specifically one with a neck that had fourteen frets clear of the body at a time when most flat tops were built with just twelve frets clear. Martin, with an eye to the wider market, christened the new guitar the "Orchestra Model."

The O.M.—as it became known—had a longer scale length than was usual for the time, and was an instant hit; unfortunately, however, it was merged after only three years with the "000" fourteen-fret neck series of guitars, which had a shorter scale length. But the O.M. guitar just wouldn't die. Its balanced sound had found popularity with solo fingerstyle artists around the world, and many luthiers began to include a version of it in their catalog by popular request. Martin finally resumed production of this model in the late twentieth century.

Remarkably, all the classic flat-top acoustic guitar designs that we love and cherish today were created in America within a decade of each other, around 1930. They have all survived

Ebony head
veneer

Ebony
fingerboard

Sitka
spruce
top

Abalone
rosette

Ebony
bridge

Waverley
tuning heads

Brazilian
mahogany
neck

Holly heel
cap

Holly
bindings

Indian rosewood
back

Indian rosewood
back

◄▲ *Kinkade Kingsdown Rosewood Deluxe is
the model constructed in this book. It has a
balanced sound and is ideal for solo playing.*

▼ *The classic Dreadnought D28
was designed by C.F. Martin in
1934, and is still the most popular
shape of guitar today.*

and are regarded as definitive in their
shapes and sizes. Many of my designs
have been developed from these
models. Using the information and
advice in this book you should be able
to adapt the plans to build any design
of your choice.

BODY SHAPES AND SIZES

The first decision you need to make
concerns the size and shape of the
guitar you're going to build. In the
nineteenth century, guitar bodies
measured as little as 12 in (305mm)
across the lower bout and were known
as "parlour" guitars. At that time these

small-bodied instruments were strung
with animal gut, although their design
can be successfully adapted to steel
stringing. They are suitable for ragtime
and fingerpicking styles of playing.

In the early 1930s, in response to the
need for a louder guitar to accompany
sung vocals, Martin introduced the
larger body shape that became known
as the "dreadnought" style of guitar.
This is the most popular shape with
manufacturers today, but you might
prefer to give your instrument a more
rounded body shape, perhaps along the
lines of the "Jumbo" designs
introduced by Gibson in the mid-1930s

▶ *Kinkade Cabot
This model is based on instruments
from the 1870s and measures
only 12 in (305mm) across the
lower bout, the largest size
available in those days. It
has a twelve-fret neck-to-
body join, a short scale length,
and wider string spacing at the bridge
for relaxed fingerstyle playing. The Sitka
spruce top and mahogany back, sides,
and neck were stained prior to
finishing in matte lacquer.
Observe how the designs of
the headstock, bridge, and
fingerboard end are all made
from straight lines and contrast
with the curves of the body shape
—a simple yet elegant and timeless
design solution.*

▲ *Larger body types, such as the Gibson Jumbo 200 shown here, are more suitable for plectrum styles of playing.*

▼ *Kinkade Clifton*
This guitar has the larger, more rounded "jumbo" body shape, 16⅜ in (416mm) wide. The top is Sitka spruce, the back and sides flamed English sycamore, and the oil-finished body is bound in English holly. The neck is laminated maple with walnut, and the fingerboard and bridge are ebony.

in response to Martin's dreadnoughts.

Designing your own shape can be quite a challenge. Experiment first with subtle adaptations of tried and tested shapes and sizes. In the captions to the illustrations I have described the finish used on each guitar, to assist you in making your decision when choosing your finishing schedule.

My model "P" is a radical shape for players looking for a distinctive, non-traditional design. The intention here was to develop a new body outline, incorporating a bridge positioned more centrally on the main part of the

vibrating soundboard, to achieve a better balance of tone. You could experiment with something similar.

Once the basics have been mastered, symmetry and convention can be ignored, as demonstrated in my Braque guitar. This instrument emerged from my fascination with the intriguing musical instruments that appear in the work of the cubist artists, including Picasso and Gris. Many artists of this period were musicians—Braque himself was an accomplished player. As a painter myself, I was unable to resist the temptation to bring one of these instruments to life.

THE POWER OF THE UNCARVED BLOCK

Many consider Michelangelo to be the greatest artist of all time; readers may be familiar with his 18 ft (5.5m) tall statue of David

▲ *Kinkade Model "P"*
Usually the waist is the tightest body curve on a guitar, but here it is on the upper bout. The large Florentine cutaway balances the body shape as well as providing unhindered access to the upper frets. The top is Sitka spruce, the back and sides figured walnut. Notice the tapered design on the headstock and scratch plate, reflecting the body shape. The bridge and fingerboard are ebony. The guitar has an oil finish.

◄ *Kinkade Cubist Braque*
This instrument was copied from the George Braque painting Bottle of Marc *(1930) which features a good front elevation of the guitar. I have "wrapped" the rest of the painting around the back and the sides. The Braque guitar has a short 18⅞ in (480mm) scale, and is tuned to G. The top is western red cedar, the back and sides mahogany, and the paint finish is acrylic.*

that is now in Florence. When Leonardo was asked the question "How could you possibly have carved a statue so magnificent as that from one block of marble?" his response was, "David was already in the block. I just chipped away the excess to allow him to escape." This is an excellent analogy for guitar building. The guitar you want to create lies within you. All you need do is trust that the corresponding structure and design is in the wood, and that you can chip away the excess to uncover it. Keep chiseling, be inspired, and have faith that you can do this.

Michelangelo also said that the greater danger for most of us is not that we aim too high and miss, but that we aim too low and succeed with ease. Follow his advice, and keep your hopes and aims as high as possible. That way you have an excellent chance of realizing your ambitions and fulfilling your own high expectations in the shape of the superb instrument you are capable of creating.

GUITAR MAKING AS THERAPY

Making a guitar is a form of self-development: it requires dedication, commitment, and, most of all, passion. That's not to say it doesn't help to have a talent for making things in your genes. My father served his apprenticeship as a toolmaker and my mother comes from a family of coachbuilders who produced the wooden bodywork for Rolls Royce cars. I believe this has made my journey as a luthier an easier one.

Perhaps the most important virtue for the luthier is patience. If you are the type of person who wants everything to happen at the drop of a hat and to your own timetable, then you are going to find building a guitar a very challenging experience.

Persevere with the stages of construction one step at a time, staying calm and focused as you move forward. Like a painter or writer you will become totally absorbed in the process. You will become the work. Your senses will be educated on many levels; your technical abilities will develop, and you will end up with a magnificent instrument.

Making a guitar also makes excellent therapy. Along the way you will learn many things, not just about guitar construction. You will learn about human behavior, especially your own. Things will not always run smoothly: there will be setbacks as well as triumphs; problems to solve as well as moments of exhilaration. How you deal with these as they occur is a measure of your progress, as a guitar maker and as an individual. Enjoy the journey.

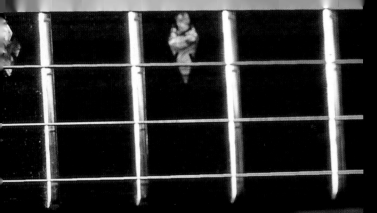

Getting Started

This section will help you to visualize the instrument you will build, and give you a comprehensive overview of the tools and techniques you will use. Although the procedures are carefully explained with accompanying photographs, the emphasis throughout is on adapting the information given to build your guitar to fit your own design and specifications.

Design

- Aesthetics
- The body: how it works
- Rosette decoration
- Bindings
- End flash
- The neck
- Headstock design
- Cutaways
- Trussrods
- Inlays
- Bridges
- Designing your own body shape

Design

◄ *Kinkade Kingsdown Mahogany Classic This variant is made with mahogany back and sides, bound in holly, while fingerboard and bridge are Brazilian rosewood. These materials create a different look, feel, and sound.*

This book guides you step-by-step through the construction of the Kinkade Kingsdown guitar. This medium-sized guitar is inspired by and derived from an old C.F. Martin design. The waist has been moved toward the neck by about ½ in (12mm) and the curve tightened below the lower bout.

The Kingsdown has an even response across all the strings, making it ideal for fingerstyle playing; it can also handle strumming and plectrum work. Because it lacks the "boominess" of larger models, it records beautifully, and is also suitable for amplification. This chapter describes the parts of the guitar, their function, and the potential for customizing some of the details.

In simple terms, a guitar is a set of vibrating strings, anchored at one end on a soundboard with an attached resonating chamber, and at the other end on a protruding neck, on which the string length, and therefore the pitch of the note, can be modified. Good design produces an instrument that has a pleasing tone, with adequate volume, sustain, and projection. It should play easily, and look attractive—factors that are of course subjective to every player.

Every element of construction has a bearing on the tone and sound quality of the instrument. Each part is a link in the energy chain, from the plucked string, through the neck and body, then back to the string. Any shoddily

constructed or ill-fitting part weakens the chain, and in doing so reduces the performance of an otherwise well-made instrument: a loosely fitted fret, for example, inhibits the transfer of vibrations from the string to the fingerboard, while a poorly seated saddle inhibits energy transfer from the string to the soundboard.

AESTHETICS

What should your guitar look like? I believe that form should follow function and my preference is for guitars that are minimally decorated and not overly bedizened. Instead I rely on proportion, resolved shapes, and the quality of the wood to endow the instrument with a timeless beauty. My guitars have no back center seam inlays because they can interfere with the pattern of the wood. But these are

choices you make for yourself. Other areas where you can easily express your individuality are in the headstock and bridge designs. Makers often create their own trademark shapes here for easy identification from a distance.

THE BODY: HOW IT WORKS

Energy from the vibrating strings is transmitted through the bridge to the soundboard, which is the guitar's main tone generator. The soundboard is internally braced to counteract the 160–175 lb (70–80kg) pull of the strings with an X-braced pattern of struts. This design, originally developed by C.F. Martin around 1850, is still the most commonly used, largely because it delivers the tone most sought after by players, and seems impossible to improve upon. The braces are shaped both to resist the pull of the strings and to transmit the sound energy efficiently, so that the soundboard is responsive to the entire spectrum of frequencies.

Sound energy, in the form of waves, is reflected by the back and sides of the body, with different materials lending their own tonal resonances to the mix. Denser materials, like rosewood, reflect sound waves more efficiently, giving greater sustain, overtones, and harmonic content to the tone of the guitar. Less dense timbers, such as mahogany, give rise to a lighter sound, which some people describe as having a "woodier tone." They also tend to create an instrument with less "apparent" string tension, and this facilitates easier playing over extended periods of time.

ROSETTE DECORATION

Various inlays or purflings (the "rosette") may be added around the soundhole, to strengthen the fragile edge and reduce the risk of splitting the soundboard. This is an obvious place to add an individual decorative touch if required, and a number of different rosette designs are illustrated above.

Only one trench has to be cut for this simple and elegant design, seen here in a natural finish **1**. A dark brown stain was applied to the soundboard and inlay of this Kinkade Cabot model prior to lacquering **2**. This single-strip inlay was masked off while a claret sunburst finish was applied **3**. Two concentric purfling strips endow the soundhole on this instrument **4**, which also features a pyramid-style bridge. A double and single black-white-black purfling looks different with and without a teardrop scratch plate fitted (**5** and **6**). Rosettes with an inlay of shell, such as abalone, make a handsome feature; its sparkling beauty provides the instrument with a stunning focal point **7**.

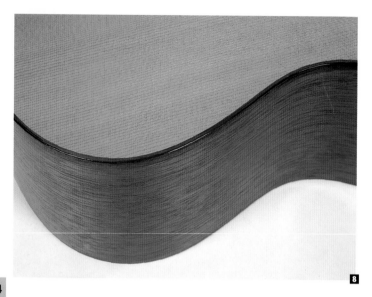

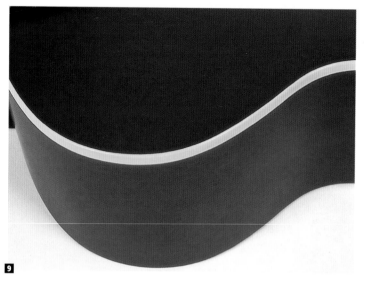

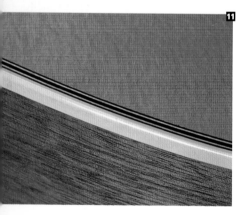

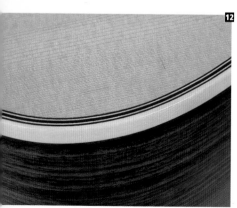

BINDINGS

Bindings are fitted to guitar bodies to seal and reduce moisture loss through the end grain. They also offer a degree of protection to the body edges and can be used to great decorative effect, dramatically changing the aesthetics of the instrument.

Binding ideas

In an example of restrained design, the binding on this mahogany guitar **8** is restricted to a single rosewood strip, and on the stained mahogany instrument **9** to a single holly strip. The back of the former is (despite appearances) left unbound **10** to add visual weight to the front binding. This instrument was made with a "Spanish style" integral neck/top block (see page 109), enabling the heel to be dressed away for comfort.

Holly is juxtaposed with a pair of black-white-black purflings for a classic look on this oil-finished, mahogany-bodied guitar **11**, as it is on this lacquered rosewood model **12**. The purflings can be substituted with an unusual crow's foot inlay **13** for a subtle change from herringbone.

Another black-white-black purfling strip can be added to the binding detail on the side **14** for extra decorative effect. Combined with an end flash, it handsomely embellishes the base of the

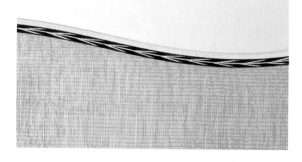

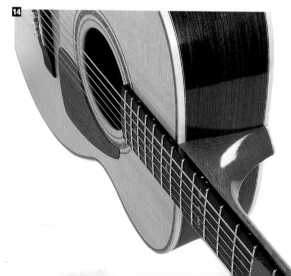

guitar **15**, here crowned with a "Parisian eye"-style endpin.

The same multiple binding sequence in holly lends a lightweight and elegant feel to this Kinkade Clifton model in flamed English sycamore **16**, **17**.

Dark edge bindings of Indian rosewood emphasize the form of this sycamore guitar **18**. A rosewood body bound in ebony, however, needs the bordering purflings to define the binding edge **19**.

This time the rosewood is bound in mahogany **20** with matching mahogany and maple purflings. Finally **21** this Indian rosewood body is bound with maple and herringbone purflings, following the American tradition.

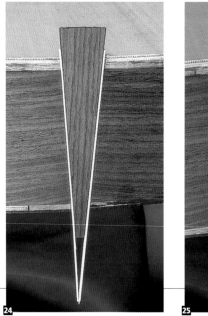
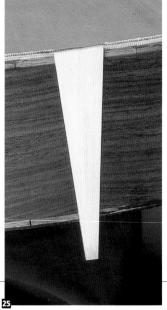

22

23

24

25

END FLASH

This can be as simple or as elaborate as you choose. It can even be left out completely: just make a neat butt join of the sides when gluing them to the bottom block. Illustrated above are a holly inlay with black purfling in walnut sides **22**; a holly inlay with multiple purflings in rosewood sides **23**; rosewood with holly purflings in rosewood sides **24**; and holly with no purflings in rosewood sides **25**.

THE NECK

Although some makers use different dimensions, the most common scale lengths in steel-strung guitar construction are: 24.9 in (632.5mm), known as "short scale," and 25.4 in (645.2mm), or "long scale." In this book we use the latter, which helps produce more volume, resonance, sustain, responsiveness, and tone in the instrument.

Custom builders can alter both the neck width and depth to suit the player's needs. You only need to add $1/16$ in (2mm) to the width of the fingerboard along its length to produce a fretboard with extra room for fingerstyle purists. Remember to add the same dimension to the string spacing at the bridge when drilling the bridge pinholes. Creating this extra width on the fretboard can enable the player to achieve difficult stretches during fingering. The extra timber in the neck may also balance the sound and deepen the voice of the guitar.

HEADSTOCK DESIGN

In design, the headstock should relate to and recall the body shape: this one perfectly matches the Kingsdown **26**.

Traditional, simple shapes are timeless and easy to build **27** and can be adapted for slot-head designs **28**. For added effect the simple shape may also

26   27   28   29   30   31

▼ *Two slices of walnut are sandwiched between layers of slab-sawn flame maple during construction to achieve this stunning effect.*

be bound **29**, and the possibilities multiply with different veneers and neck materials **30**, **31**. You could even omit the head veneer altogether **32**.

More complex headstock designs take varying forms, from adaptations of the Gibson classic **33** and art-deco styles **34**, to tapered designs that allow the strings to pass through the nut with less deviation, reducing the friction and potential tuning problems **35**, **36**. A volute on the back of the headstock helps resolve a number of different curves at their juncture **37**. It can be an attractive feature, although some players find its presence a hindrance for certain first position chord shapes. I think it does little to strengthen the neck at this potential weak point.

Headstock angles

Over the years guitars have been made with various headstock angles, up to a maximum of 17 degrees. Increasing the angle creates more downward pressure at the nut and "apparent" string tension, delivering a brighter tone from the strings. But it also increases friction in the nut and tends to weaken the headstock-neck area due to an increase in short grain exposure.

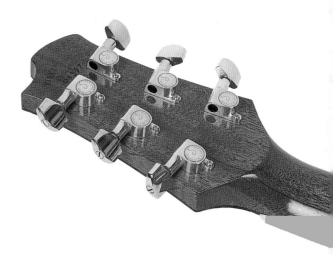

37

32 **33** **34** **35** **36**

38

39

40

▼ *Venetian Cutaway*
The rounded cutaway creates a
pleasing effect, combined with .
the pyramid bridge design and
straight rather than curved
fingerboard end. The back
and sides are of mahogany
and the guitar is finished in
gloss cellulose lacquer.

CUTAWAYS

Cutaways afford the player unrestricted access to all of the fretboard and can be either Florentine **38** or Venetian **39** in profile. They are complex to construct: considerable skill is needed to achieve a flush junction at the heel and the edge of the fingerboard to the sides. When bending sides into extreme curves, the timbers can be thicknessed down to $\frac{1}{16}$ in (1.5mm) in that area.

TRUSSRODS

A trussrod is installed in the neck to reinforce it against the forward bowing effect caused by the tension of the strings. Many trussrod designs have been invented: the guitar in this book uses one that is adjusted through the soundhole. Other designs are adjusted via a coverplate on the headstock face, installation of which involves removing additional material from the neck **40**. I avoid this approach, as it reduces strength in an already weak area, and impedes energy transfer from the string anchor point on the headstock through to the neck and body.

◄ *Florentine Cutaway*
A Florentine cutaway allows comfortable access to the whole
fingerboard. The back, sides, and neck of this guitar are flame
maple, complemented by a rosewood binding, and finished in
matte lacquer. A bound maple head veneer and diamond
mother-of-pearl fingerboard inlays complete the picture.

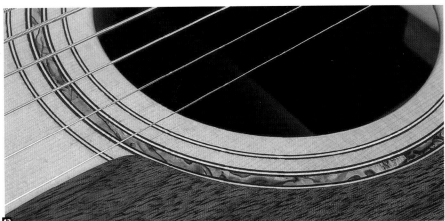

INLAYS

Inlaying natural shell products adds further embellishment to your guitar. Many shapes, such as diamond position markers  and segments for the rosette , are available ready-cut.

The hybrid instrument shown at right has an inlay scheme derived from its art-deco style, and utilizes both mother-of-pearl and abalone on the soundhole cover , fingerboard , and bridge . These inlays were all cut by hand. An inlay on the headstock adds an elegant finishing touch to any instrument .

BRIDGES

The shape of the bridge can be easily adapted. Keep to the approximate size on the plans and observe other guitars for inspiration. The pyramid-style bridge illustrated above **47** is a Martin design dating back to the early nineteenth century. It is a challenge to make neatly: simple shapes are easier to execute **48**. Pinless designs are neat and comfortable to use if you damp the strings with the heel of your hand, but they are harder to make and may afford less scope for adjustment **49**.

DESIGNING YOUR OWN BODY SHAPE

If you're the adventurous type you can design your own body shape. Take time over this process: as a novice it is easy to fall in love with your initial ideas, which may later turn out to be hopelessly impractical, or just not very good. Begin by making a cardboard cutout of your sketches. Mock-up the soundhole, bridge, fingerboard, and headstock with contrasting dark colored material where relevant. Hang it up and observe it for a couple of weeks. Inadequacies of shape should become obvious over time; for example, where the curves just don't balance. Go back to the drawing board and rework it. Make another model and hang that up, again observing it over a period. Remember there are significant differences between the curves of a body drawn appealingly on a white sheet of paper and what that shape actually looks like when translated into three dimensions.

If you do decide to create your own shape, you will need to take account of the following technical adjustments. Referring to the plans, retain the relationship of the fingerboard to the bridge for accuracy of intonation, and that of the bridge to the bracing pattern. For small bodied guitars,

▼ *Kinkade Acoustic Bass*
*The design of the six-string acoustic guitar can be
scaled up and adapted to create an acoustic bass.
The body shape of this one is designed to
accommodate the 34 in (864mm) string length. It is
18 in (458mm) wide and 5½ in (140mm) deep. The
top is Sitka spruce with mahogany back and sides.
The bass can be made in both fretted and fretless
versions. This four-string has a matte lacquer finish.*

▲ *Kinkade Resonator*
*The resonator guitar was designed in the mid-1920s
by the Dopyera brothers, to deliver more volume.
Some originals were made with nickel-plated
bodies, sandblasted with patterns and Hawaiian
landscapes. The Kinkade interpretation has a body
in solid flame maple with the pattern applied by
lightly spraying through a stencil onto a sunburst
matte lacquer finish.*

reduce the thickness of the soundboard
to about ⁷⁄₆₄ in (2.5mm) when using
Sitka spruce, and the back to ⁵⁄₆₄ in
(2mm) when using rosewood. On
larger-bodied guitars, the soundboard
thickness can be increased to ⅛ in
(3.2mm) in the middle. The bracing
heights could also be reduced by
⁵⁄₆₄ in (2mm) in smaller guitars and
increased by the same dimension in
larger-bodied instruments.

▲ *Kinkade Glastonbury*
*This hybrid instrument is powered by both
piezo and magnetic pick-ups. It is constructed
from a hollowed-out mahogany body—dug-
out canoe style—with a Sitka spruce front.
Notice that the soundhole has been moved to
a position on the upper bout. This area of the
soundboard has only been considered by
luthiers as a suitable position for a soundhole
since the late twentieth century. This guitar
has a matte lacquer finish.*

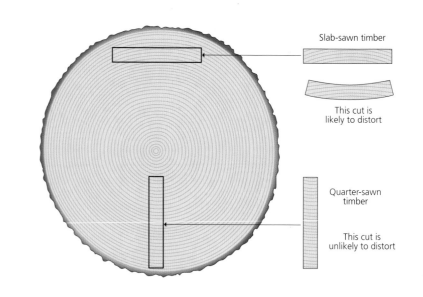

Slab-sawn timber

This cut is
likely to distort

Quarter-sawn
timber

This cut is
unlikely to distort

Materials

■ **Quarter-sawn wood**

■ **What wood where?**

■ **Hardware and fixings**

■ **Adhesives**

■ **Abrasive papers**

One of the delights of building guitars is that it involves working with wood, the most marvellous of natural materials. No two pieces of wood are exactly the same. The grain patterns, textures, and qualities of the different species are limitless in their variations.

If you source your wood from a luthier supply shop, it will have been cut, prepared, and dried by those who understand the qualities that luthiers look for. Different species will have been sorted, graded for quality, and priced accordingly. You should be able to obtain all your materials by mail order, confident in the knowledge that you will receive exactly what you ordered. But there is much to be said for selecting your own pieces. All luthiers have their own preferences and build their instruments in their own unique fashion.

QUARTER-SAWN WOOD

Wood is a hygroscopic material: it absorbs moisture from the atmosphere and gives it out again—even after

proper seasoning—like a sponge. This causes the wood to expand and contract, and this expansion and contraction takes place at differing rates, depending on the aspect of the grain to the surface of the wood. Quarter-sawn wood—that is, wood obtained from a cut perpendicular to the tree's annual growth rings—has optimal grain orientation (see diagram above), and is less likely to distort than slab-sawn or other cuts, making it our preferred choice for guitar-making.

Splitting billets for soundboards

Soundboards are ideally made from billets of split material, and top grades of spruce are produced when slices are removed from a split surface of quarter-sawn wood. This means that as well as being perpendicular to the end of the board, the grain also runs through it, and this has the effect of imparting greater strength.

Another feature luthiers look for in spruce is close grain lines, indicating a

slow-grown tree. The closer (or tighter) the grain, the stiffer the board; the stiffer the board, the better.

Bookmatching

The soundboard and back of a guitar are constructed from jointed boards that are cut from consecutive slices of wood. This means that when joined, they form a pattern that mirrors itself, just like an ink-splat painting. The sides are also prepared in this manner.

Quality of wood

Whether you buy the highest grades of wood for your first guitar depends on your woodworking experience and the tools available. You might find some species of hardwood tougher to work than others. Generally, the higher grades have a more even grain pattern that facilitates easier hand planing. It is probably advisable to select medium-grade pieces until you are more confident.

Salvage is another possible source of wood. Several of my early guitars were

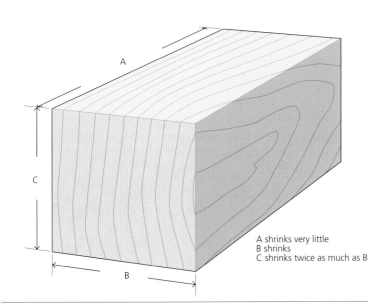

A shrinks very little
B shrinks
C shrinks twice as much as B

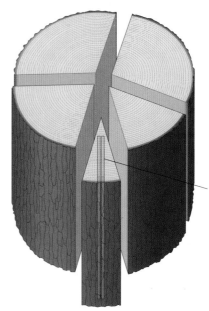

Soundboards cut from split billets

made from planks removed from rubbish skips. Wood reclamation yards are worth investigating, and suitable quality wood can be found in old furniture and fittings from building refurbishments. Woods of this age are bound to be well seasoned, and can be used even if they are not quarter-sawn, since they will be extremely stable.

Whatever wood you use, always keep the offcuts, since they often come in useful further along in the construction process: for example, for testing finishes and adhesives.

Tapping for tone

You will find references in this book to tapping parts of the guitar and listening to the tone produced. The process starts here, during wood selection. It is not complicated. If you hold one of the halves of a soundboard by its end and rap it lightly with your knuckles, you should hear a bright and lively response, indicating a rapid transfer of frequencies through the wood. A dull, soft, soggy tone indicates a poor piece that should be rejected. A visual inspection of the grain pattern generally reveals which pieces will have the best tone. However, pieces with wider grain patterns can often sound good and will make terrific soundboards. This tapping can also be done when selecting backs, sides, and other wooden parts.

WHAT WOOD WHERE?

Wood is chosen for its acoustic as well as its aesthetic qualities, and the species selection has a pronounced effect on the tonality of the finished instrument. This section describes the acoustic and aesthetic properties of some of the more commonly available tonewoods.

Soundboards

Spruce has always been the preferred wood for soundboards, whether on violins, pianos, mandolins, or guitars. Qualities to look for are a close, straight grain, stiffness across the grain, how well it is quarter-sawn, and its tap tone.

◄ Bookmatched wood is used for the soundboard, back, and sides of the guitar. If the pieces are well prepared, they will form a perfect mirror-image of each other.

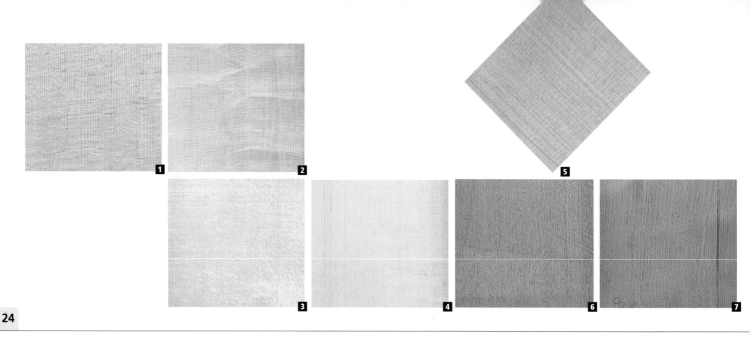

Materials

Sitka (*Picea sitchensis*) **1** is the toughest member of the spruce family, and is particularly suitable for steel-string guitar construction. Its color ranges from cream to pinkish brown. Some Sitka spruce shows a marking in its grain know as hazelfichte or "bear claw" **2**. This naturally occuring figure appears as swirls across the grain, and is generally thought of as a desirable feature, both for its appearance and because it can make the board stiffer.

Sitka spruce makes an instrument that responds well to all styles of playing.

European spruce (*Picea abies*) **3** is sourced from the alpine region of Europe. These forests have been logged for centuries and mature trees are scarce, so quality wood is more expensive than Sitka, and difficult to find in pieces rendered from split billets. Grain patterns are wider and the color is always an even, lustrous white or ivory. Some luthiers believe European spruce gives greater harmonic content.

Englemann spruce (*Picea engelmannii*) **4** is creamy white in color, perfectly even, and close-grained. It is softer and less strong than Sitka, so use it 5–10 per cent thicker. It is thought to impart extra sparkle to the tone of an instrument and is good for

◄ *Kingsdown Brazilian Rosewood Deluxe*
This oil-finished example is made with an Englemann spruce top and Brazilian rosewood back and sides. The latter timber is often a dark chocolate color, but this guitar is built using a mid-tone figured set and looks gorgeous. Notice the light streak of sapwood that creates an attractive feature in the center of the back.

fingerstyle uses, although I prefer Sitka for hard playing.

Western red cedar (*Thuja plicata*) **5** is a gorgeous warm orange color and comes from trees of huge girth. It has a bright tone, with excellent attack; it lacks a certain depth, but this suits many players. It is not as strong as spruce, although it is stiffer across the grain. It marks easily, so must be worked with great care. Cedar soundboards should be 10–15 per cent thicker than their spruce equivalent.

Back and sides

The back and sides are sold in quarter-sawn, bookmatched sets. Brazilian rosewood, Indian rosewood, mahogany, and maple have been the traditional favored choices of luthiers, although any even, close-grained hardwood can be readily substituted. All of the above-named are widely available with the exception of Brazilian rosewood, which is now an endangered species.

Mahogany (*Swietenia spp.*) **6** is the least dense of the woods commonly

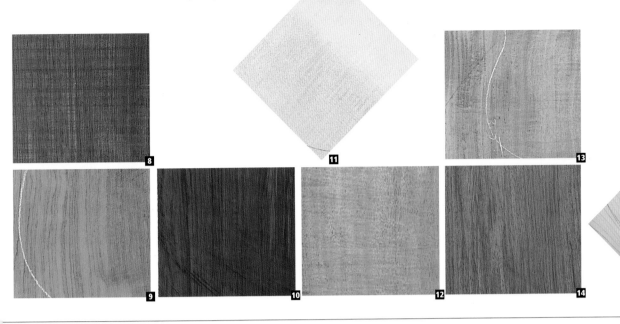

used for guitar backs and sides. It is very easy to work with hand tools and this makes it a good choice for your first instrument. Prepare the back a little thicker than you would rosewood, to around ⅛in (3mm). Figured mahogany **7** is more expensive and is harder to plane without chipout due to the rising and falling grain pattern. The piece illustrated comes from Brazil.

Indian rosewood (*Dalbergia latifolia*) **8** is used on most top-grade instruments. It is a dense material and is tough to hand plane to thickness, although side-bending is usually straightforward. Colors range from purple-browns to reddish browns and it sometimes has red or orange streaks. This is a top grade set.

Brazilian rosewood (*Dalbergia nigra*), the densest of all rosewoods, used to be considered the premium choice for back and sides. Thanks to overlogging, however, it is now unobtainable except from old stock, and what little there is sells at exorbitant prices. It varies in color from milk-chocolate **9** to a rich dark brown **10**.

Maple (*Acer saccharum*) **11** has been the traditional choice for instruments of the violin family since time immemorial. Prized for its curly figure, it is a mid-density wood with excellent acoustic properties. It is a challenging material to work: prone to chipout during hand-planing due to its rippling grain pattern, it also likes to "unwind" during side bending, and highly figured pieces can fracture around tight curves.

Koa (*Acacia koa*) **12** hails from Hawaii, and is both expensive and extremely attractive, with better grades exhibiting distinct flame. It is a medium density wood and produces a beautiful guitar with a fine tone. Tasmanian blackwood (*Acacia melanoxylon*) **13** is a cousin to koa and very similar, with gorgeous color and grain patterns, including flame in higher grades.

American black walnut (*Juglans nigra*) **14** is slightly denser than mahogany and is gaining in popularity. It is easy to work and bend and has fine tonal characteristics. It is sometimes available with streaky color and flame patterns.

English yew (*Taxus baccata*) **15** is a dense hardwood traditionally used for making longbows. It is suitable for guitar making but is hard to season without cracks and shakes.

▲ *The Kingsdown Cutaway (below) has a flamed maple back, sides, and neck, while the Kinkade Model "P" (above) is made from American black walnut with a Brazilian mahogany neck.*

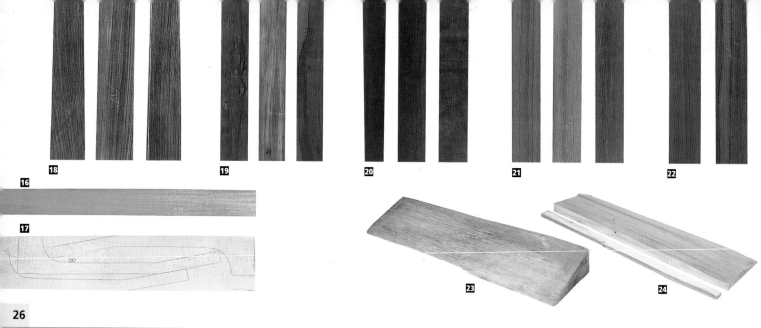

Materials

Necks

Mahogany **16** is the most commonly used neck wood. It is easy to work and adds warmth to the tone of your guitar.

Maple **17** is harder than mahogany; it makes a stronger neck and imparts a brighter edge to the instrument's tone, but takes considerably longer to hand carve. A maple neck looks best on instruments with maple back and sides.

Fingerboards

Your choice of fingerboard material also affects the tone of your guitar, though not as much as your choice for the back and sides. Indian rosewood **18** is the most common. It is stable and relatively easy to hand-plane and fret, making it ideal for a first guitar.

Brazilian rosewood **19** is dense and oily, and adds a sparkle and a ring to the guitar's sound. Partnered to great effect with a mahogany back and sides, it is now increasingly difficult to buy. I will miss its unique tone, stability, and resistance to wear.

Ebony (*Diospyros spp.*) **20** is hard wearing but difficult to work by hand. It has a deader tap tone than the rosewoods and this dampening effect makes for a smooth sound. It is a good partner to rosewood, and other dense timbers.

Madagascar rosewood (*Dalbergia greveana)* **21** is an alternative to Brazilian rosewood and has a similar effect on the tone. It is mostly available in an orange color and is easy to work.

Bolivian rosewood (*Machaerium scleroxylon)* **22**, also known as Santos rosewood, morado, or pau ferro, is a dense, easily worked wood, purplish tan in color and streaked with brown or black figure.

Brace wood

Braces cut from split billets of spruce are best for strength and tonal transfer **23**, **24**. The quality and elasticity of the brace material is as important as that of the soundboard: test the springiness of each piece before you buy.

Kerfing

Makers variously use spruce, lime, mahogany, or basswood for kerfing; I prefer mahogany. The photograph shows differently designed kerfings **25**.

Top and bottom blocks

Mahogany is a good choice for blocks —notice how they are cut from the board **26** to achieve the correct grain orientation. Some makers use spruce, basswood, or even plywood for this job.

Bridges

Rosewood and ebony are the most suitable woods and will impart their qualities in much the same way they do when used as fingerboard material. The examples shown here are made from Indian rosewood **27**, Brazilian rosewood **28**, and ebony **29**.

HARDWARE AND FIXINGS

There's more to a guitar than planks of wood, no matter how beautiful or well seasoned. Here are some of the extra bits and pieces—from bindings, to bridge saddles, to fretwire—you need to construct and finish your instrument.

Binding materials

Plastics—black, white, tortoiseshell, or ivoroid—are all used, as are woods of various kinds. Shown here are (from left to right) ebony, Indian rosewood, holly, walnut, koa, flame maple, box, and mahogany **30**.

Purflings

Purfling strips **31** are available from luthier's suppliers in a range of different patterns.

Inlay materials

A broad range of pre-cut inlay shapes is obtainable from luthier's suppliers in either mother-of-pearl **32** or abalone **33**, which exhibits a range of colors from reds and blues, to greens and purples.

Alternatively you can create your own shapes, from mother-of-pearl or abalone blanks, from more unusual materials like malachite, turquoise, and coral, or from one of a number of reconstituted shell materials **34**.

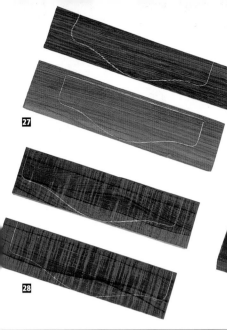

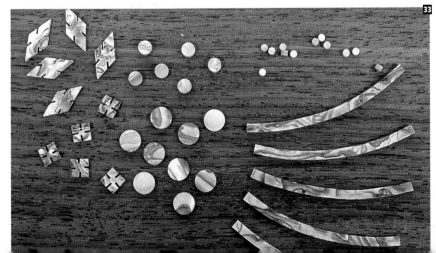

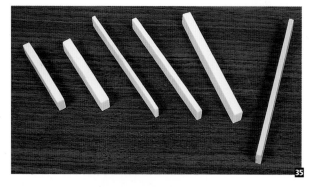

Nuts and saddles

Bone is a natural material and imparts a bright tone. It comes in pre-cut blanks for nuts and saddles **35**. Micarta is a hard, dense plastic, useful when fitting under-saddle pick-ups that are suffering because of the uneven density of bone.

Fret wire

This is made from an alloy of copper, zinc, and nickel for corrosion resistance. It comes in many sizes and several degrees of hardness, either in a coil or straight lengths **36**.

Bridge pins and endpins

Plastic bridge pins **37** come in black, white, and cream finishes with mother-of-pearl or abalone eyes. Endpins **38** are made from ebony or rosewood and may have mother-of-pearl dots or "Parisian eye" patterns.

Tuning Machines

Always buy the best tuning machines you can afford. Consider the weight of the heads since they will have an effect on the balance of the instrument. Smaller-bodied guitars made with mahogany back and sides should have lightweight sets. All makes are available in chrome, nickel, and gold finishes.

ADHESIVES

Luthiers have a wide range of choice from the many specific-use adhesives available to the woodworker today.

Aliphatic resin

AR glue is used for virtually all construction work **39**. It "grabs" fast, cures quickly, sets hard, and is resistant to thermoplastic "creep." It is also water-soluble for easy clean up.

Hide glue

The traditional choice for centuries, hide glue is available ready-mixed **40** and in granule form **41**. The granules are dissolved in water in a hot glue pot. The glue is best made fresh daily, and is easily dismantled using hot knives.

Cyanoacrylate

Better known as superglue, this adhesive was developed for battlefield surgery—which is why it sticks fingers together so well **42**. The gel type is useful for gap filling and inlaying, while the thin variety makes excellent emergency chip repairs during construction. Always use with extreme caution: ensure adequate ventilation; wear eye protection; and follow the manufacturer's instructions.

Plastic cement

This is used for bonding plastic bindings to wood **43**. Test on your chosen plastics before use.

Contact adhesive

Useful for bonding abrasives when making sanding sticks (see page 35)—do not use it on your instrument **44**.

Epoxy resin

Available in a number of different varieties with different setting times, epoxy resin **45** makes a good gap-filler when mixed with fine sawdust. I also use it for the center join on oily rosewood backs.

I do not recommend using general woodworker's white (PVA) glues as the joints are likely to "creep" in time.

ABRASIVE PAPERS

Made from different materials, and available in a range of grades, there is an abrasive paper to suit every task.

Garnet paper

Cheap and cheerful **46** and suitable for intermediate stages of wood finishing.

Waterproof silicon carbide paper

"Wet-and-dry" **47** is used dry for the final sanding of wood and fret-finishing work, and wet for cutting back lacquer.

Aluminum oxide paper

This is a harder-wearing, clog-free paper for finishing, available in sheets **48**, cloth-backed rolls **49**, and strips **50**.

Silicon carbide paper

Equally hard-wearing and clog-free **51**, and available in finer grades than aluminium oxide paper.

Micro-mesh paper

This high-tech, cloth-backed abrasive **52** is available in extremely fine grades (up to 12,000) for polishing lacquer finishes.

Tack rag and wire wool

Tack rags **53** are used for cleaning surfaces before applying lacquer. Wire wool **54** polishes frets to a high shine or creates a satin finish on lacquer: 0000 is the finest grade available.

Tools

- **Conventional woodworker's tools**
- **Specialist tools**
- **Tools you can make**
- **Handheld power tools**
- **Machine tools**

Conventional woodworker's tools (screwdrivers, vises, clamps, hammers, hand saws, and pliers) are employed for much of the guitar-building process. In addition, however, the guitar maker requires a number of specialist tools. When purchasing these pieces it makes sense to buy the best quality you can afford. Don't hesitate to ask your supplier for detailed information about the performance and behavior of a product, and avoid brands aimed at the home improvement market. Keep your tools sharp: that way they are more controllable and therefore safer.

CONVENTIONAL WOODWORKER'S TOOLS

Clamps

A guitar maker cannot survive without a vast array of clamps. Collect various sizes for different procedures **1**.

Vise

As well as a large bench-mounted vise, you will also need a portable vise for smaller items **2**.

Bench plane

A good second-hand bench plane, like the Jack plane illustrated here **3**, is perfectly adequate for guitar making. Having worn the old blade away with continued sharpening, I replaced it with a Japanese laminated type of blade. The extra-hard steel of the cutting edge is supported by softer, more durable steel. It is good for spruce and mahogany, but the extra hardness makes it brittle, and its lack of durability shows when planing ebony and rosewood.

Toothed blade

This can help reduce chipout when planing highly figured timbers **4**. Simply file the cutting edge of an old blade into small segments with a needle file prior to sharpening.

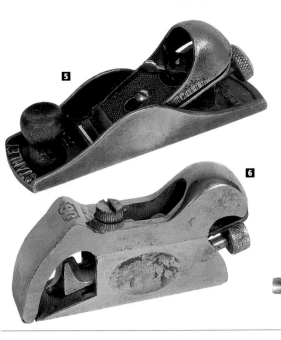

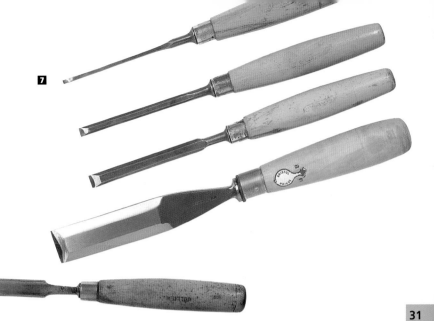

Block plane

Once again, perfectly good planes can be bought second-hand **5**. Before you buy a plane, compare a new one with an old one. Look at the flatness of the sole and the quality of the blade. The original blade for this plane is long worn out and it is now fitted with a blade made by a specialist luthier toolmaker. The blade has been hardened to 60 Rockwell, and can be honed to a beautiful edge. It is extremely durable.

Shoulder plane

Use this tool with its nose removed when planing the back of a headstock to thickness **6**.

Chisels

A well-balanced chisel is a joy to use. I prefer bevel-edged chisels **7** to the straight-edged variety. The higher the quality of the steel, the better and longer they'll hold their edge. You will use the 1 in (25mm) chisel most often. Other useful sizes are ⅜ in (10mm), ¼ in (6mm), and ⅛ in (3mm).

Gouges

Not an essential tool but useful when carving neck volutes and trussrod access in headstocks. This 1 in (25mm) gouge **8** gets most use when I'm carving arch-top guitars.

Knives

Knives are useful tools for fine and accurate work. The modelmaker's varieties have replaceable blades **9**. The luthier's knife **10** is more robust.

Cabinet scrapers

Three different shapes of cabinet scraper are shown here, together with a "sharpening kit"—a file and screwdriver shaft **11**. This is an incredibly useful tool, simple but effective, for finishing timber. Sharpening the scraper is described on page 42.

Rasps

Rasps are useful for shaping necks **12**. The photograph shows a new type, made with a collection of hack-saw blades—coarse on one side and fine on the other—and a conventional model. The home-improvement style of rasp is very efficient for removing large quantities of material quickly **13**. Many luthiers use spokeshaves and draw knives for shaping necks.

Files

Assorted files **14** are useful for shaping jobs, especially with nuts and saddles.

Coping saw

This saw **15** is used to cut curved lines. It is useful for headstocks or for the outline of the front and back if you don't have access to a band saw.

Fretting saw

A fretting saw **16** can be used for similar purposes as the coping saw. It has a deeper throat providing greater access in some applications. For more delicate work it is fitted with much finer blades.

Piercing saw

This jeweler's tool **17** is fitted with blades so fine that it is hard to see which way the teeth are set. It is used for cutting out mother-of-pearl shapes.

Straight-edges and rulers

A 24 in (600mm) straight-edge **18** is an essential piece of equipment, used specifically for checking the straightness of a surface. A selection of steel engineering rules are prerequisites for accurate measurement.

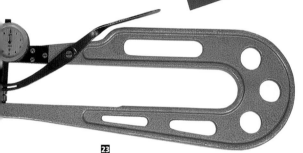

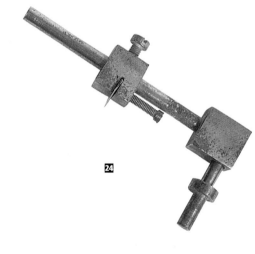

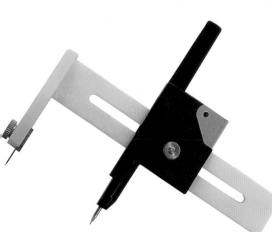

Square and sliding bevel

The square **19** is used to check that surfaces are at 90 degrees to each other. The sliding bevel is used to check angles that are not square.

Sharpening stones

All cutting tools, especially planes and chisels, will only work satisfactorily if their cutting edges are razor sharp. Many varieties of sharpening stone are available. Shown here **20** are a combination India oil stone (right) and a diamond grinding stone (left).

SPECIALIST SAWS

The saws illustrated here **21** are (from top to bottom):

Back saw

This is used for cutting fret slots and producing a slot of accurate width.

Gents saw

Used for hand-cutting dovetail joints and other small jobs.

Micro saw

This is also used for cutting fret slots.

Modelmaker's back saw

Used for preparing braces for the soundboard.

SPECIALIST TOOLS

Hygrometer

This tool **22** keeps tabs on the humidity levels in the workshop—critical information for the luthier.

Dial-gauge calipers

These calipers **23** are used for measuring thickness, particularly the thickness of the front, back, and sides during preparation. The tool measures to an accuracy of $\frac{1}{256}$ in (0.1mm).

Circle-cutting tools

These tools **24** consist of a blade that rotates in a compass, and are used for cutting the trench for rosette inlaying. You could easily make your own.

Bending iron

This solid aluminum former is heated internally by electrical elements **25** before the sides of the guitar are bent against it (see page 79).

Fretting hammer

The head is a jeweler's chasing hammer and the shaft here **26** has been added after the original proved inadequate. Don't use it for banging in nails as this will mar its polished surface.

Fret press

This is the tool for seating frets and is supplied with brass cauls of differing radii **27** to suit the camber of the fretboard.

Fret snippers

This tool **28** is used to neatly snip the ends of the frets flush to the edge of the fingerboard.

Fret stone

A coarse- and fine-sided sharpening stone **29**, used for fret dressing.

Fretting files

A triangular file with its edges ground is my favored fret crowning tool, and is shown here **30** together with a set of nut-slot-cutting files.

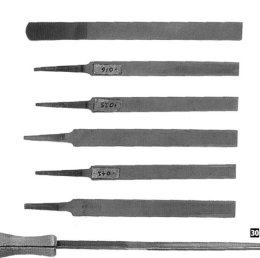

Reamer

You can easily create a tapered
bridge pinhole with this tool **31**.

TOOLS YOU CAN MAKE

Calipers

To save the expense of buying a set,
calipers **32** can be quickly fashioned.
The pencil is wedged in position to a
known depth and when the calipers
are drawn across the work, the high
areas will be marked.

Wooden cam clamp

These cam clamps **33** are not hard to
make, and can exert considerable
pressure, saving you much expense.

Sanding sticks

Glue abrasive material to a stick to make
a useful and versatile shaping tool **34**.

Purfling cutter

This alternative to a router for cutting
rebates for purflings and bindings has
a blade made from a broken hacksaw
blade, spaced by shims to produce the
correct depth of cut **35**, **36**. In my
experience it is more controllable than
tools sold for this purpose.

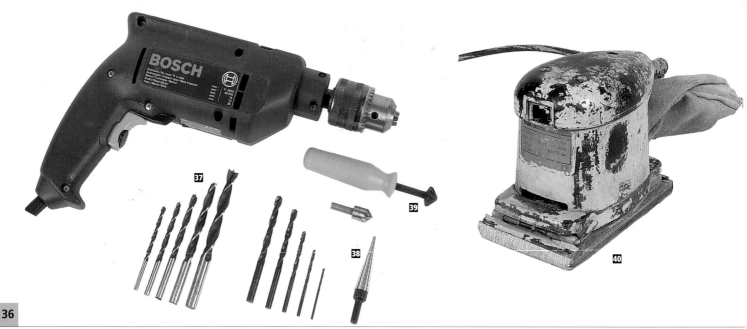

HANDHELD POWER TOOLS

Electric drill and bits

Brad-point drill bits **37** are self-centering and reduce chipout on their entry to a surface. The step drill bit **38** is a useful gadget for enlarging holes accurately and without chipout.

Countersinks

I use countersink bits or hand countersinks **39** to create a nice beveled edge on bridge pin holes, and on any hole drilled in a lacquered surface.

Palm sander

This small mechanical sander **40** is a useful aid in finishing work.

Orbital sander

This larger sander **41** might come in handy if you make a mess of the hand planing when preparing the soundboard and back.

Router

Having several routers saves constantly resetting them for different tasks. The lightweight machine shown here **42** is fitted with a flush-cutting bit, used for trimming the soundboard and back flush to the sides after gluing. The more powerful model **43** has template guides and two sizes of collet to fit various cutting bits.

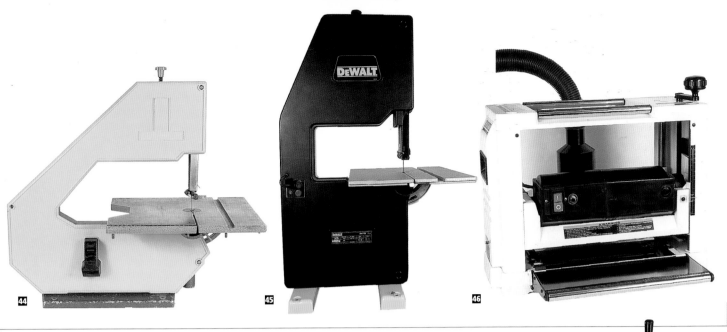

44   45   46

MACHINE TOOLS

Small band saw

The three-wheel lightweight band saw **44** is fitted with a fine blade, making it suitable for delicate tasks such as cutting the soundboard and back outlines.

Larger band saw

Larger saws **45** are capable of accurately cutting through 4 in (100mm) mahogany, but are still light enough to move around the workshop.

Bench-mounted planer thicknesser

This portable machine **46** is a real time-saver when preparing the soundboard, back, and sides. It is more gentle on the wood and does not have the dramatic "after-bite" of larger machines. Use it only on the best grades of timber, and don't attempt to remove more than 0.01 in (0.25mm) per pass. Do not use it on lower-grade wood, especially anything with knots, or severely rising and dipping grain, such as figured woods—bear claw spruce, flame maple, and flame koa. Stop at $\frac{3}{64}$ in (1mm) over the desired thickness, or if the grain is ripping out, and drum-sand or hand-finish to final thickness.

Power sander

This single-drum cantilevered model **47** is shown with its dust cowl lifted so you can see how the abrasive is wound onto the drum. This tool makes the thicknessing process easier, faster, and more accurate. It is especially useful when working on highly figured woods because the grinding process never causes chipout of the grain.

Drill press

A pillar drill **48** makes accurate drilling of holes exceptionally easy. It is very useful when preparing various jigs, for example tuning-machine hole jigs.

Bobbin sander

A bobbin **49** can be attached to a drill press or radial-arm saw, and is used when preparing the mold.

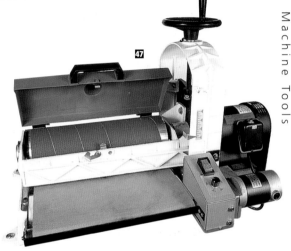

47

48   49

Good practice

- **Making notes**
- **Order of construction**
- **The workshop environment**
- **Tool sharpening**
- **Remaining in a state of awe**

The guitar-building processes described here are based on "traditional" construction techniques. These have been thoroughly tried and tested over years and decades and, in my experience, result in quality instruments with soul and great tone. Our primary interest is not in labor-saving shortcuts, but in building guitars to the highest possible standard without compromise. This chapter includes general guidelines on preparation and techniques that you should find useful as you build your instrument.

MAKING NOTES

It is good practice to make notes as you build, especially as you reach the final stages of the soundboard, back, and sides. Record details of dimensions—the thickness of the soundboard in different areas, and brace heights and widths—and of the techniques and methods used, both successful and unsuccessful. In six months time, when you start making your second guitar—this is an addictive business—you'll have trouble remembering exactly how you did everything. You won't want to be peering inside your first instrument, trying to remember how you shaped the braces.

As well as the physical dimensions of the guitar, write down what you

▲ It is important to keep detailed notes, of dimensions for example, and of any problems that may have arisen while making the guitar.

thought of the quality of the wood. Was it AAA grade? Was it the stiffest piece you could find? Or was it slightly softer? What was the tap tone like at each stage? Make as many notes as you can, so that later on you'll have valuable reference material to hand.

You could also use a camera to record each stage. This will give you a visual aide-memoire of significant aspects, such as the way you scalloped the braces—a record of what went on inside your guitar for future occasions. It will also serve to impress your friends and relations when you show them the finished instrument. Don't underestimate the fascination this exerts: many of my customers come to visit me during construction to photograph the various internal parts of their guitar, before they disappear from view forever.

◄ Photographing each stage, especially the insides, can be a helpful reference when you come to make another guitar.

ORDER OF CONSTRUCTION

For the sake of clarity, and to make them easier to follow, the step-by-step instructions in this book are ordered into chapters named after parts of the guitar. It is worth noting that I do not actually build my guitars in exactly the step order shown here. For example, in practical terms I thickness the soundboard, back, and sides at the same time. Then I start work on the neck and fingerboard. Then I return to working on the body parts. In this way I allow one part of the instrument to settle while I work on another. Gradually I am able to bring all the pieces together. You can ad-lib throughout the process as you see fit. Common sense will tell you which stages cannot be done before others—such as attaching the neck before binding the body.

THE WORKSHOP ENVIRONMENT

Make sure your working environment suits your particular personality, and that your workshop becomes a place of retreat and serenity, one where you feel at home. Remember that a beautifully sculpted instrument is going to emerge from this space.

Site your workbench in an area that is lit by both natural and artificial light. Gooseneck lamps are useful for this purpose. My main workbench is situated in front of a window with an opaque blind that I can pull down as necessary  to control the amount of light in the room. Ideally your bench should be positioned at the correct

3

height for your stature and bolted to the wall for extra stability.

Spend some time planning your storage options. Walls can be used to hang guitar molds **2**, while shelves and small drawers are useful for keeping bits and pieces handy and free of dust **3**. You can also use the area below your bench to store tools **4**.

HUMIDITY

Relative humidity is defined as the amount of moisture contained in the air as a percentage of the maximum amount of moisture the air is capable of holding at a given temperature. Due to its hygroscopic nature, wood will continue to move even after your guitar has been constructed. An increase in humidity will cause the wood to expand and a decrease will cause it to shrink.

A guitar can cope with a moderate increase in humidity; this results in the wood swelling, which causes the soundboard and action to rise. A severe drop in moisture levels, however, will cause structural damage such as cracks and splits in the soundboard and back.

Your work area must be kept at a controlled humidity level. My advice is to build your guitar in an environment with humidity levels slightly lower than those where the instrument will ultimately reside. A workshop humidity of 40–45 percent and a temperature of about 70 degrees (21 degrees Celsius) is ideal. You can achieve these conditions by using a dehumidifier, and by heating the room when necessary. An instrument constructed in this way should be capable of handling changes in humidity during travel or touring.

4

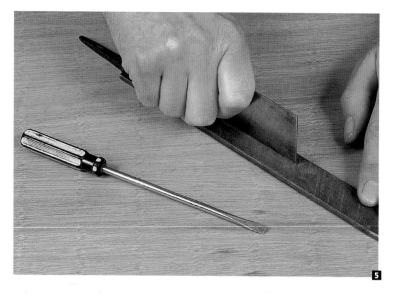

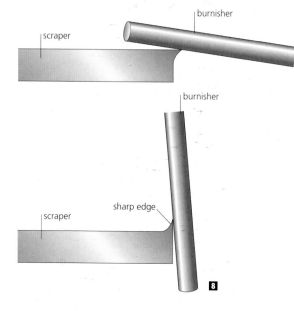

TOOL SHARPENING

Here are a few pointers to keeping your tools in good working condition.

Cabinet scraper

A burr is created on the edge of this tool, enabling you to remove fine shavings from timber and leave a smooth surface. To sharpen it, first rub the edges that are to receive the burr on a single-cut file, making sure that you hold the scraper perpendicular. This cleans off the worn-out burr and squares up the edge **5**. Draw a burnishing tool along the edge of the scraper, creating a burr on the edge of the steel **6**. Turn the burr over to form the cutting edge **7**, **8**.

Plane and chisel sharpening and setting

Check the flatness of the sole of the plane **9** and remedy if necessary by grinding on coarse abrasive paper or on plate glass with grinding paste. The plane blade is sharpened in two stages: initially by grinding at an angle of 25 degrees on a grinding wheel, and then

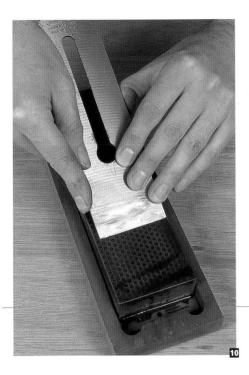

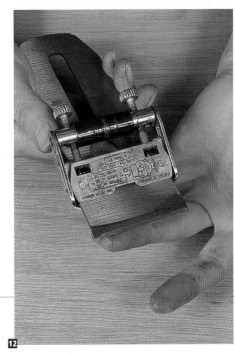

by honing the cutting edge to an angle of 30 degrees by hand-holding on a grindstone **10**. This does require practice and you might find a honing guide useful, especially if you do not have a mechanical grinder. Using the honing guide, set the blade to 25 degrees and grind the cutting edge on coarse stone. Reset the blade to 30 degrees in the guide, and grind on a fine-grade stone **11** until you can feel a burr develop on the flat back side of the blade's cutting edge **12**. Remove the burr by lightly pushing the blade sideways against the stone on the blade's flat side **13**. This should create a razor-sharp edge. I have ground a slight curve on the outside edges of my blade **14**, which enables me to cut a shaving without digging into the wood at the extreme edges of the blade's width.

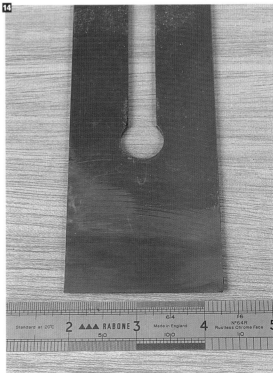

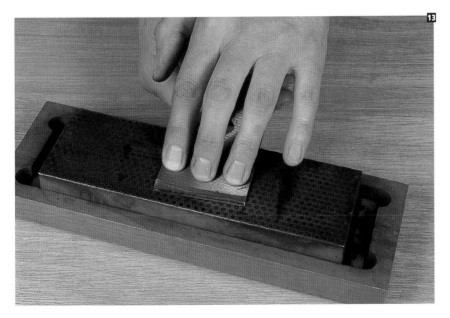

HEALTH AND SAFETY ISSUES

Some people develop allergies to certain hardwoods, such as rosewood and ebony. The dust they produce is probably not good for us anyway, so you should always use a dust mask when sanding.

It is also important to wear ear and eye protection when using any machine tools. Avoid wearing loose clothing, and make sure that long hair is tied back. Keeping your workshop tidy at all times will do much to prevent accidents.

Reassemble the cap iron close to the cutting edge **15**. Sight down the sole of the plane, and adjust it so that the center part of the blade is showing parallel to the sole **16**. Then retract the blade. Gradually increase the depth of the blade during use until you achieve the size of shaving you want.

Always plane with the direction of the grain—the grain lines "lean" away from you. If you plane in the other direction the blade will dig into the timber causing tears and chipouts on the surface. You should also remember to plane away from your body whenever possible.

You might like to experiment by varying the honing angles on your tools

between 25 and 35 degrees while working on softer and harder timbers respectively. The larger the angle, the stronger the cutting edge.

Chisels are sharpened in exactly the same way as plane blades.

Kinkade Tip

Remember to sharpen your tools as soon as they have lost their edge. Blunt tools cut inefficiently, causing chipouts and inaccurate work. They are also much more difficult to control, which puts your safety at risk.

REMAIN IN A STATE OF AWE—KEEP ASKING QUESTIONS

There are 101 ways to make a guitar. This book guides you through just one: a way that works for me, and has the approval of my customers. The more guitars I make, the more my knowledge of the process increases—and I have been doing this day in, day out for nearly three decades. Just when I think I've got it off, along comes an unfamiliar problem. Every single day I discover something new about the behavior of stringed instruments. I have long since come to the realization that I will never know everything.

Reiner Maria Rilke, the German poet and mystic, urged us to "Live the questions now. Always be a beginner."

This is excellent advice. Remaining in a state of awe and wonderment allows us to be open to new and sometimes better ways of doing things. Believing we have all the answers closes us down and prevents us from discovering exciting developments and possibilities. So I urge you to keep on asking the questions. If you get stuck at any stage, ask for help from people who have been there before, and learn from their mistakes. That is how luthiers develop their art and skill—by sharing experience, strengths, and hopes.

Developing a meditative state

To be productive as a guitar maker you need to create a sense of balance and harmony in your life. You cannot make a guitar under pressure. You need a calm mind. Don't work on your guitar when you feel rushed or stressed; you will make the wrong decisions, some of which could have dire consequences for your instrument or your sanity.

There will be moments when you feel consumed or confused by the process—this is when you need to take some time out. Walk away from the project for a while; stop and make yourself a snack or a hot drink. You will soon regain perspective. When you return with a calm mind, things will seem clearer. You will be better able to rectify problems. This should prevent you making unnecessary mistakes.

Making a guitar is not a task for the fainthearted, and neither can the process be rushed. Take regular breaks. The whole adventure is going to take as long as it takes. Work slowly and carefully and concentrate on improving efficiency. Allow yourself to become lost in the process. In due course, and almost despite yourself, the end result will materialize. It will not disappoint.

Building the Guitar

This part of the book sets out the entire construction process. Comprehensive directions, clear photographs, and instructive artworks guide you step-by-step through every stage of building and assembling your guitar, from making the mold, to finishing and setting-up.

Building the Guitar

The Mold

- **Transparent template**
- **Solid mold**
- **Semi-solid mold**
- **Workboard mold**
- **Jigs and templates**

The construction of any stringed musical instrument is made easier and more accurate if you use a mold, or former, to hold the various parts firmly in position while you work on them. Making a mold takes time, and impatient readers might feel they'd rather dispense with this stage and get on with making the guitar itself. Trust me when I say that a good mold is a valuable investment of your time, facilitating easier operations and more efficient clamping procedures later on.

Mold-making can be approached in a number of different ways, each of which has particular advantages and drawbacks. I have outlined three methods of construction below: choose the one that best suits the tools and equipment you have to hand. They are all exterior molds; that is, the guitar is built within them. Although they happen to be fashioned from solid wood, plywood, or particleboard, there is no reason at all why they could not be constructed from other materials, such as plastic or glass fiber resin. If you

1

have skills in these areas you could make a much less weighty version.

TRANSPARENT TEMPLATE

Whichever type of mold you make, you must start with an accurate template of half your body shape **1**, as determined at the design stage (see pages 12–21). A cardboard template is easily cut with scissors but a more durable pattern can be made from clear acrylic plastic. This has the added benefit of transparency, invaluable when selecting wood.

SOLID MOLD

This heavy mold **2** is extremely durable and could well outlive you! Relatively straightforward to make if you have access to a large band saw and a bobbin sander, the mold separates into two halves to facilitate easy release of the guitar body. During construction, the halves are connected at each end with a wooden "strap."

The mold is constructed from eight pieces of 1 in (25mm) thick plywood or

2

3

MDF **3**, each measuring 24 x 10 in (600 x 250mm), and two pieces of scrap wood for the straps. Stack four of the boards, and glue and screw them together. Transfer the guitar shape from the template, aligning edge to edge **4**. Repeat with the remaining four boards to make the opposite half of the mold **5**. Cut inside the line on the band saw **6**, then bobbin sand down to the line. Make the connecting straps and fasten at both ends before truing up to the line at the ends where the two halves meet **7**. Trim the excess wood to reduce weight **8**, leaving a border of at least 2 in (50mm). Sand the inside of the mold smooth with a rasp or a bobbin sander **9**.

4

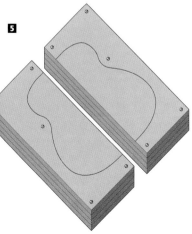

6

8

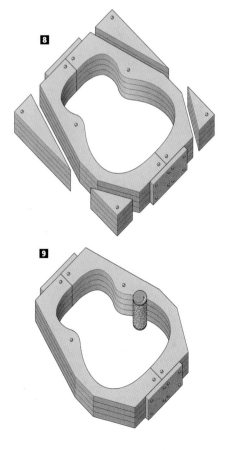

5

7

9

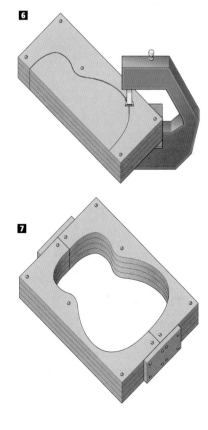

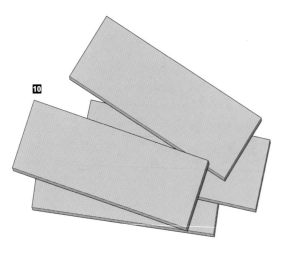

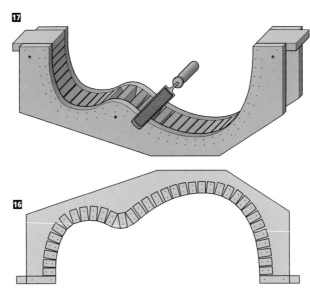

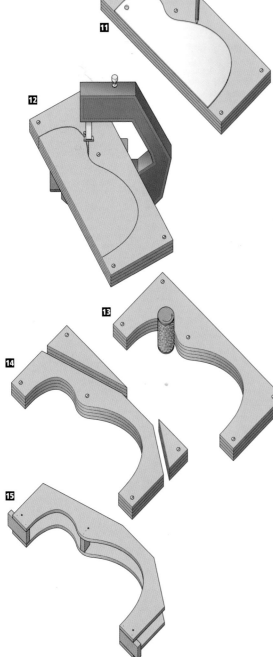

SEMI-SOLID MOLD

This is the type of mold I favor, and the one featured in this book. It is made from plywood shapes separated by softwood spacers. Like most guitar-making methodology, it was designed to take advantage of the tools and equipment available to the maker at the time. Take four pieces of ¾ in (18mm) thick plywood **10**, each measuring 24 x 10 in (600 x 250mm). Transfer the guitar shape from the template to the plywood, aligning edge to edge **11**. Cut each piece out one at a time on a band saw, or stack all four together, screwed away from the line, and cut them out on a larger band saw, remembering to cut inside the line **12**. Bobbin sand the shapes back to the line **13**. You now have two pieces for each side of the mold and are assured of symmetry. Trim excess wood from the outer edges of the boards **14** to leave a border of at least 2 in (50mm).

The spacers are made from 2 x 1 in (50 x 25mm) prepared softwood, accurately cut to 3 in (75mm) lengths on a radial saw or by hand with a miter box. Two pieces of plywood are used where the two halves butt together, and the protruding ends of these pieces are screwed together to join the halves.

Start by gluing the two plywood end spacers in position, together with one softwood spacer at the waist **15**. Position them slightly proud of the surface of the curve, and hold in place with panel pins while the glue sets. Do this on a flat surface and check their alignment with a set square. When dry, glue the remaining softwood spacers in place, proud of the surface **16**. When the glue has set, trim the spacers back to the edges of the plywood using a rasp and sanding blocks **17**. Finally, align the two halves and fit the joining screws **18**.

Stop blocks for solid and semi-solid molds

Stop blocks effectively decrease the depth of the mold, allowing the sides to protrude to enable the fitting of the top and back. Make ten stop blocks as

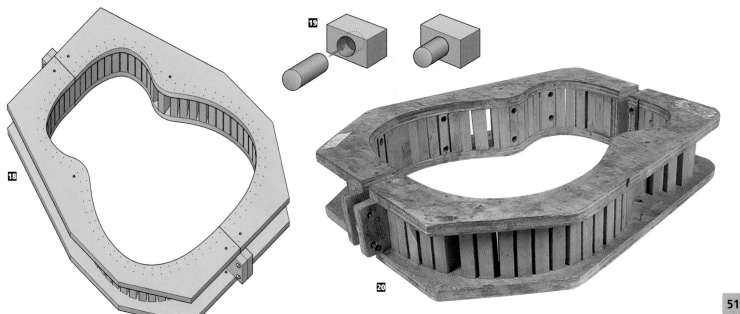

follows: cut a 1⅛ in (28mm) length of
¾ x ¾ in (18 x 18mm) softwood. Drill a
½ in (12mm) hole centrally in one face
to a depth of ½ in (12mm). Glue a 1 in
(25mm) length of ½ in (12mm) dowel
into position **19**.

Mark "front" on one face of the
mold and "back" on the other. Draw a
line on the inside of the mold, 1 in
(25mm) from the front face. Drill ten
½ in (12mm) holes evenly spaced along
the line to accept the stop blocks **20 21**.
The other set of holes on the back edge
will be made when the side taper has
been created.

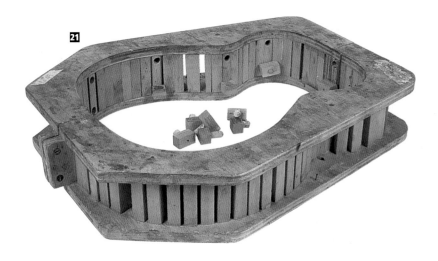

Side-tapering jig for solid and semi-solid molds

This jig—shown from above **22**, below
23, and in position on the mold **24**—
guides you when cutting the sides of
the guitar, which taper on their back
edge by ⁹⁄₁₆ in (15mm): they are parallel
from the bottom block to the widest
part of the lower bout, then narrow to
the top block in a graceful curve. The

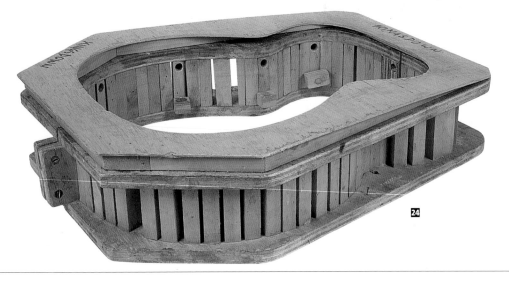

Kinkade Tip

Cutaways can be accommodated in a standard mold by making an insert that is temporarily screwed to the mold from the outside.

jig is made from ⅛ in (3mm) plywood with shaped batons glued to its underside.

Clamping caul for solid and semi-solid molds

The caul creates even pressure on the perimeter of the soundboard and back when gluing them to the sides. This one is made from ⁵⁄₁₆ in (8mm) plywood, routed in the center portion to ⅛ in (3mm) **25**. This gives it flexibility to conform to the curvatures of the soundboard and back, while retaining stiffness at its edges. Alternatively you could use a single thickness of ⅛ in (4mm) MDF. Cut the caul 1¼ in (30mm) larger than the body shape. Drill 22 holes at even spaces around the perimeter for 2 in (50mm) no.10 screws to fix the caul in place when clamping.

WORKBOARD MOLD

This is a quick and easy mold that I use for custom shapes and one-offs. Draw the centerline on a 1 in (25mm) plywood or MDF board big enough to

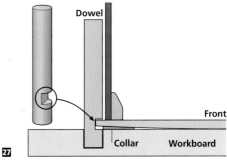

accommodate the guitar body shape. Then mark around the template on each side of the center line. Drill twenty ½ in (12mm) holes, each about 2–3 in (50–75mm) apart and ½ in (12mm) deep, around the perimeter line. Cut twenty 3½ in (90mm) lengths of ½ in (12mm) doweling, and insert in the holes. These posts will support the sides while the guitar is being constructed **26**—though not as securely as do either of the previous two molds.

A recess cut in the base of the posts accommodates the oversized soundboard as the sides are glued onto it **27**. There is also a cardboard collar, 1 in (25mm) wide and ⅛ in (3mm) thick, which prevents the soundboard's domed shape being crushed during this procedure. The posts are merely pushed into the holes, not glued, enabling easy release of the sides and soundboard after gluing **28**.

Gluing the top and bottom blocks to the sides is a slightly more tricky operation with this system because you do not have a ready-prepared caul to clamp them against. Improvise with flexible plywood and small batons. When gluing the sides to the downward-facing soundboard, pressure can be effectively created by several clamped or weighted transverse bars.

With this method, the process of trimming the side tapers needs to be performed more delicately as there is little support for the sides, so go very gently. When gluing the back onto the sides, pressure can be created with adhesive tape, if the back is trimmed close to the sides, assisted with

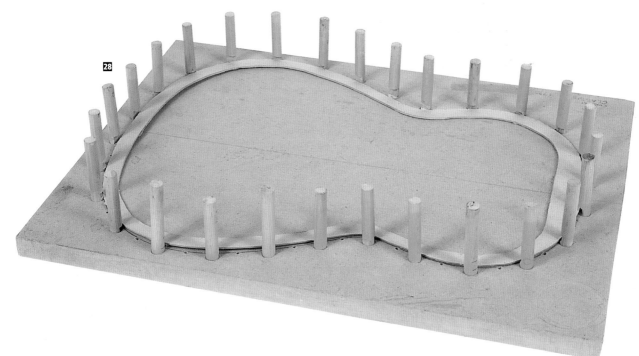

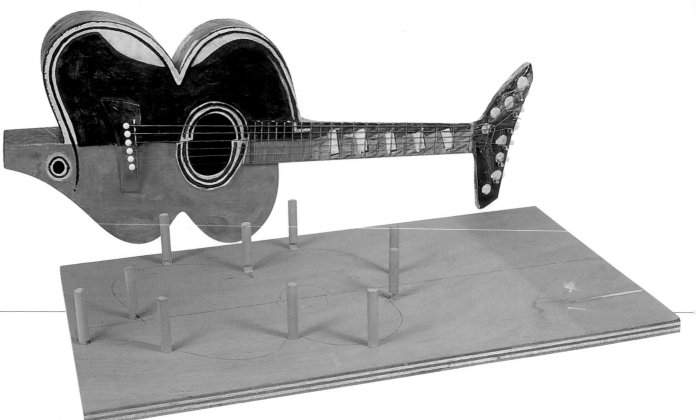

29

clamps and cauls at top and bottom block positions.

This workboard mold can be extended at the neck end to facilitate Spanish-style guitar construction. In this method the neck is integral with the top block, and the sides simply fit into a slot. The neck, soundboard, and sides are glued together at the same time, avoiding the complex dovetail neck joint of steel-strung guitars. This type of mold is ideal for one-off designs, such as an asymmetrical body shape **29**. With its Spanish-style integral neck-to-body join, it is a fine example of eccentric luthier's art.

JIGS AND TEMPLATES

Like the mold, there are some other useful tools and "formers" that can be made to aid the construction of the guitar.

Workboard

The workboard is simply a 24 in (600mm) square of ¾ in (18mm) plywood, used to prepare the soundboard and back. You will also need a longer workboard, 40 x 8 in (1000 x 200mm), for making the sides.

Shooting board

The shooting board is a stepped board, used for joint-making on the soundboard and back. The workpiece is laid on the top step and clamped firmly, while the plane is used on its side to create a perfectly square and true edge, avoiding plane wobble.

Guitar-holding jig

This device holds the guitar safely and securely while various operations are carried out **30**. The headstock is clamped to a swiveling plate, with the neck resting on the cradles. The body is supported by wedges of foam.

Go-bar press

This is an ancient method of exerting pressure during gluing. Flexible bars of ash, approximately ½ x ⁵⁄₁₆ in (12 x 8mm), create pressure as they are confined in a space shorter than their length **31**. They bear on a concave dish, and matching curved struts are pressed and glued in the press onto the soundboard or back, creating a domed structure. Most amateur luthiers will rarely encounter such a device, although you may find yourself making one if guitar-making becomes a serious hobby.

30

31

Curved template

To create a curved line, place thin card on the workboard and nail two molding pins the desired distance apart in a straight line. Mark the center point and the desired depth of the curve. Push a uniform dimensional bar, wood or metal (or, as here, carbon-fiber neck reinforcing stock) against the pins, bending it to the depth mark. Draw along the curve with a 3H pencil **32** **33**. Cut around that line and you have a template to trace from. By varying the depth marks and the spacing between

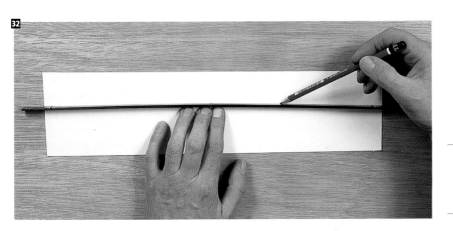

32

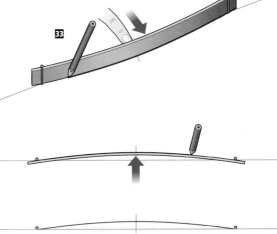

33

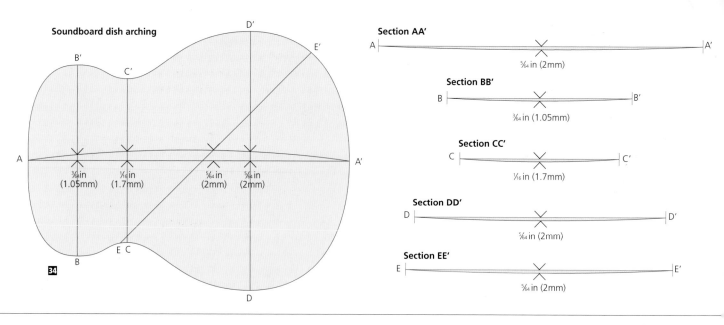

Soundboard dish arching

Section AA'
⁵⁄₆₄ in (2mm)

Section BB'
³⁄₆₄ in (1.05mm)

Section CC'
¹⁄₁₆ in (1.7mm)

Section DD'
⁵⁄₆₄ in (2mm)

Section EE'
⁵⁄₆₄ in (2mm)

³⁄₆₄ in (1.05mm) ¹⁄₁₆ in (1.7mm) ⁵⁄₆₄ in (2mm) ⁵⁄₆₄ in (2mm)

34

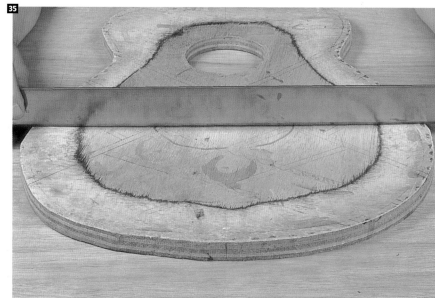

35

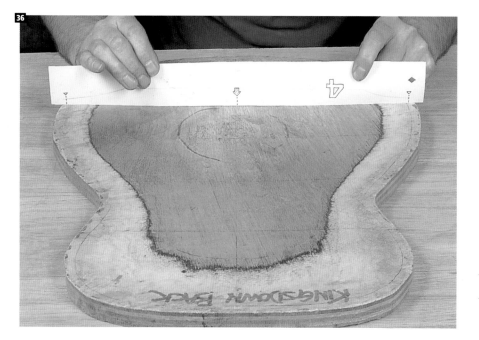

36

the nails you can create any curve and thereby make all the curved templates you need for the soundboard and back braces **34**.

Go-bar dishes

If you decide to deviate from the plans given here—to give a different arch on your soundboard, for example —you can calculate the curves of the braces and clamping dishes by using the above system and drawing full-size plans and cross-sections. If the maximum depth of the soundboard arch is ⁵⁄₆₄ in (2mm) at the bridge position—section AA' shows the depths at various points—you can plot sections BB', CC', and DD'. Then plot contour lines from this information and rout depth-guide steps into a shaped ¾ in (18mm) plywood blank. Join the contour steps with gouge, scraper, and sanding blocks to make even curves in the dish **35**. Create the brace arching templates in the same way, checking they match the curve of the dish **36**.

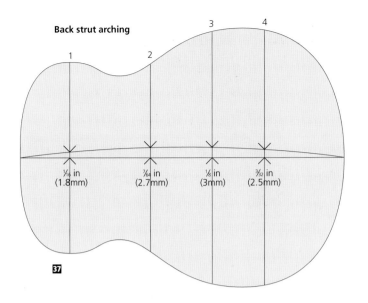

Back strut arching

1 — ¹⁄₁₆ in (1.8mm)
2 — ⁷⁄₆₄ in (2.7mm)
3 — ⅛ in (3mm)
4 — ³⁄₃₂ in (2.5mm)

37

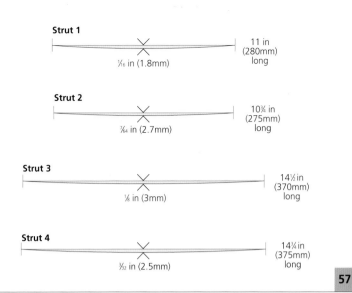

Strut 1
¹⁄₁₆ in (1.8mm)
11 in (280mm) long

Strut 2
⁷⁄₆₄ in (2.7mm)
10¾ in (275mm) long

Strut 3
⅛ in (3mm)
14½ in (370mm) long

Strut 4
³⁄₃₂ in (2.5mm)
14¾ in (375mm) long

The go-bar dish for the back has a maximum depth of ⅛ in (3mm). Use the same method for calculating and constructing. Alternatively, make four separate clamping cauls that match the strut positions 1, 2, 3, and 4, which can be used without the go-bar press but with regular clamps **37**.

You could of course avoid going to all this trouble by making the soundboard completely flat. Straight struts can be clamped to a flat surface **38**. Use the back clamping cauls process that is described above.

Clamping bar

This bar **39** has a curved edge and is used during the soundboard and back jointing processes. When faced downward and clamped at each end, the bar exerts pressure evenly along the length of the joint.

Neck cradles

Make these cradles and cauls to provide support when working on the guitar or clamping down frets **40**.

39

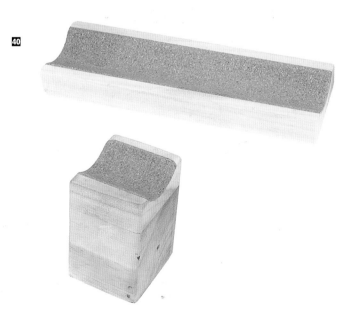

38

40

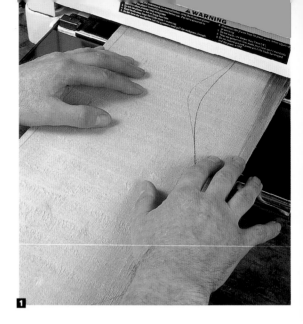

1

The Soundboard

- **Jointing**
- **Thicknessing**
- **Rosette inlaying**
- **Bracing/strutting**

The soundboard is probably the most important element of the guitar in terms of its influence on the quality of the instrument's tone. As such, it is the most delicate and complex component to build, and presents the biggest challenge. It consists of a bookmatched, jointed panel of split, quarter-sawn spruce, about ⅛ in (3mm) thick, with a decorated soundhole. A complex pattern of carved spruce braces on the reverse of the soundboard both resists the pull of the strings and distributes the energy of their vibration in an efficient manner to create the desired tone from the finished instrument.

You are about to breathe life into the wood you have selected to make your soundboard, so you need to develop an affinity with it. The closer the connection you make with the wood at this stage, the more energy and care you will put into the making of your guitar. Go slowly through the stages described and do not continue to the next step until you are absolutely satisfied with what you have done up to that point. Breathe deeply and often. Stay calm and relaxed, and, if possible, undisturbed throughout the process.

JOINTING

The two halves of the soundboard are joined with a perfect joint, one with no visible gaps. A homemade press is then used to apply pressure on the joint while the glue sets.

Preparing the rough boards

The rough-cut slices of quarter-sawn Sitka spruce are supplied at between ³⁄₁₆ and ¼ in (5–6mm) thick. Your first task is to clean up the surfaces in order to be able to inspect the grain pattern, reducing the thickness along the way. If you have access to one, then a planer-thicknesser is the ideal tool for the job. Put each board through the planer and reduce to no less than ⁵⁄₃₂ in (4mm) **1**. If not, the pieces can be jointed and glued at the thickness you receive them from the supplier, and reduced to the desired dimensions by hand at a later stage.

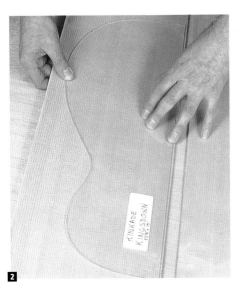

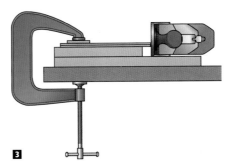

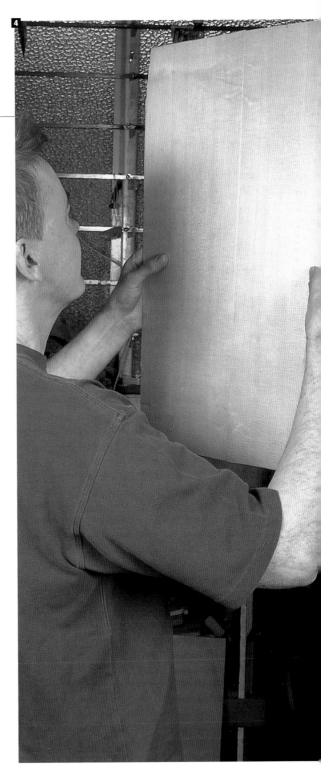

Choosing the grain orientation

View the cleaned-up boards through the transparent template and carefully inspect the grain pattern for flaws. Select the best area of the board, choosing the part with the tightest grain to be the jointing edge **2**. This becomes the center line. Mark the joint edges for identification and trim them to make the grain lines as parallel to the edge as possible.

Making the center joint

Take a hand plane with a freshly honed blade. With the boards clamped on the shooting board and the plane on its side **3**, plane the two faces of the joint until they are absolutely straight and true. Use a metal straight-edge to check your line, and inspect the surface for any flaws uncovered in the wood. Unclamp the boards and hold the jointing edges together against a window or strong light source to check the accuracy of the joint **4**. If the joint is a good one you should not be able to detect even the slightest chink of light

showing through. Repeat the planing process with one board at a time if necessary, truing each edge until you achieve a perfect light-tight joint with no visible gaps.

Making a baton-and-nail press

The joint should be kept under light, even pressure while the glue sets. You can make a press to do this using a baton and nails. Lay two or three strips of newspaper underneath the joint area on the workboard, to isolate the glue

Kinkade Tip

Tap each of the boards before gluing, listening to the tone it produces. You will be doing this regularly throughout the construction process, tapping and listening to detect subtle changes in tone. The note produced at this stage is relatively high. When the two boards are joined the tone will drop dramatically in frequency because the soundboard has doubled in size.

and ensure you don't bond the soundboard to the workboard. Place a ¼ in (6mm) baton along the center of the workboard and set the two boards on it, jointing the edges together. Hammer five nails at regular intervals into the workboard along the outside edge of each soundboard half **5**. The compression created when the baton is removed and the boards lie flat will secure the setting joint **6**.

Make a light pencil mark on the soundboard halves next to two opposite nail positions. This will help you to locate the boards in the correct position when the joint is reassembled after the glue has been applied.

Gluing and clamping

Working away from the workboard, apply a liberal amount of AR glue to one of the jointing edges **7**. Now hold the edges together and gently slide one piece against the other to distribute the glue evenly across both surfaces.

With the baton laid along the centerline, use the pencil marks to locate the two soundboard halves in position on the workboard and against the nails. Slide the baton out and carefully press the soundboard down to bring the pieces into compression **8**. The more glue you see squeezed out, the more confident you can be that your joint is good. Quickly wipe away

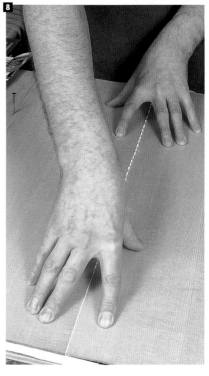

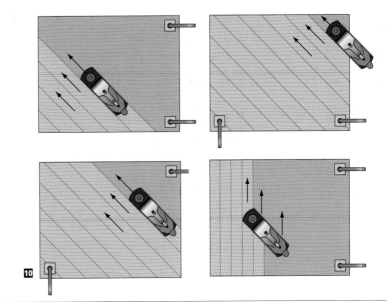

all the excess glue on the top surface. Lay two to three more strips of newspaper over the joint before clamping, using a board and clamping bar to spread the pressure evenly **9**. Leave it to dry overnight.

THICKNESSING

The soundboard is now reduced to its final thickness, our aim being to end up with a smoothly sanded and scraped surface ⅛ in (3mm) thick. This can be achieved by hand, using a bench plane, or by machine, using a power sander.

Hand planing

Thicknessing the soundboard by hand saves you the outlay on expensive power tools. It also gives you a deeper understanding of your wood, allowing you to become more familiar with its grain structure and density.

Planing spruce is a relatively swift process because the material is so soft. Using cauls, clamp the soundboard onto a clean workboard. You need to use two clamps on the work at all

times, otherwise the soundboard will rotate and twist under the pressure of the planing action, possibly marking the underside of the board. Rotate the clamps to gain access to all areas of the soundboard. Work methodically from one end to the other, reducing the thickness evenly as you go **10**. Planing across the work using a diagonal shearing action will avoid the likelihood of splintering or chipouts **11**. Plane one

side to a smooth surface, evening out the gluing line. Then turn the board over and plane the other surface in the same way.

Checking thickness

Check the thickness of the board regularly as you go using dial-gauge calipers **12**. When you get to %4 in (3.5mm), inspect both sides for evenness and identify the best surface.

Kinkade Tip

Spruce is among the softest of woods and the tiniest bit of swarf can leave a dent in its vulnerable surface. For this reason the workspace must be kept immaculately clean when carrying out operations on the soundboard. Each time you turn it over make sure that the bench or workboard below is completely cleared of dust, chippings, and any other foreign matter.

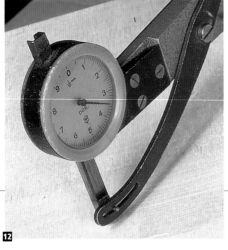

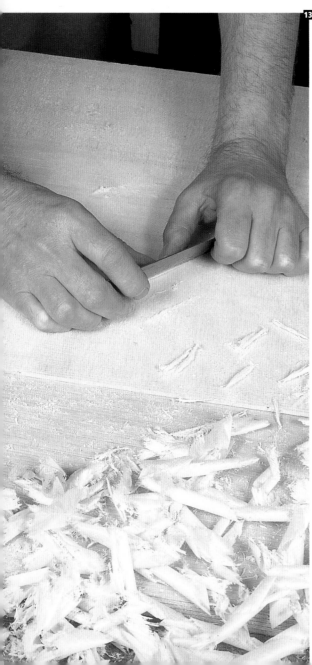

Select the surface with the finest figure and the fewest imperfections, and mark it to identify it as the outside. Continue planing the inside surface, reducing thickness to ⁹⁄₆₄ in (3.2mm), and keeping the outside surface intact. Check for "tearout" (the loss of tiny wood fibers from the surface) as you go by looking at the board at a slight angle against a strong light.

Use a cabinet scraper and sanding blocks to make the final reduction in thickness to ⅛ in (3mm) . This evens out any roughness left by the plane and leaves a perfectly smooth surface.

Machine sanding

You may feel that life is too short to hand-thickness your soundboard. The alternative, if you're lucky enough to have access to one, is a power sander— I use a cantilevered single drum model. A power sander saves time, ensures accuracy, and leaves a flawless surface.

Prior to putting the board through the machine, remove any excess glue from the joint with a scraper: this prevents it from gumming up the sanding drum. Start sanding with 80 grit, moving to 100 grit to finish off. Don't be tempted to speed things up by using a coarser abrasive: anything less than 80 grit will scar the surface.

Remove the material in multiple passes, taking off ¹⁄₂₆₄ in (0.1mm) on each pass . The sander cuts most efficiently if the wood is presented with its grain at a slight angle to the drum. Check the thickness regularly with calipers, and change to 100 grit when it reaches ⁹⁄₆₄ in (3.5mm). Now select the outside surface, make another three passes, then remove the board from the sander. Finish down to ⅛ in (3mm) using a cabinet scraper and sanding blocks, as described above.

ROSETTE INLAYING

A rosette can be anything you want it to be. In the American steel-strung tradition it's a series of concentric circles. On classical guitars it's a piece of mosaic. Installation is the same whatever the format: a trench is cut in

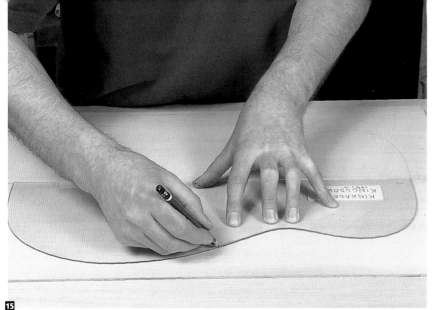

Kinkade Tip

Work very lightly when marking lines on spruce. If you press too hard with your pencil you could leave an irreversible dent in the wood.

the soundboard to about one-third of its depth, into which the chosen material is glued. The top of the inlay is left proud while the glue sets, then trimmed flush to the soundboard.

Marking the outline of the guitar

Take an HB pencil and mark the center line on both sides of the soundboard. If you've made a good bookmatched joint this can be difficult to spot: look closely at the end grain of the board for a trace of glue to help you locate its position. Place the transparent template on the outside surface of the soundboard and, using the template as a window, choose the area that reveals the best grain pattern and the fewest flaws. Align the template edge on the center line and trace around it with a 2B pencil to transfer the shape of the guitar to the soundboard. Flip the template over and trace the other side .

Marking the rosette position

Place the soundboard on a clean workboard and clamp it firmly to the bench. Using the point at which the neck meets the body as your datum point, refer to the plans and mark the center of the soundhole $5\frac{13}{16}$ in (148mm) down the center line from this point. The soundhole is $3\frac{15}{16}$ in (100mm) in diameter: mark its upper and lower edges on the center line. Put a panel pin in the center of the soundhole; this is the center point for the rosette-cutting jig. Seal the board in this area with a quick wipe of shellac or sanding sealer to reduce grain tearout as the trench is cut.

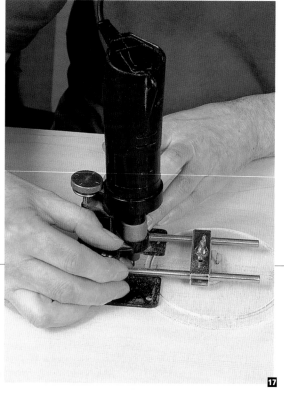

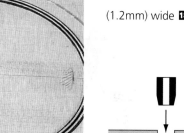

A simple rosette

Set the depth stop on a miniature router to 1mm and cut two trenches in the soundboard using a dental burr or straight cutting bit . The inside trench is 4¹³⁄₃₂ in (112mm) in diameter and ⁵⁄₃₂ in (4mm) wide, to accommodate two black-white-black purfling strips that are each ⁵⁄₆₄ in (2mm) wide. Reset the tool and cut the outer trench of diameter 5⁵⁄₁₆ in (135mm) to accommodate a single black-white-black purfling strip that is ³⁄₆₄ in (1.2mm) wide.

Cut the pieces of purfling to length, bevel the bottom edges to facilitate ease of entry, and mark them. Apply gel superglue copiously to the trench and in between the layers of purfling. Gently tap the purfling into place and hold it down with some weights, using a sheet of newspaper to isolate the glue. Leave to dry for one hour.

Remove the central panel pin, and use a cabinet scraper to scrape the purfling back flush to the soundboard. Take care to avoid denting the surface of the spruce.

A deluxe rosette

This more complex style of rosette uses exactly the same processes, but incorporates a gorgeous New Zealand Paua AbLam inlay. After four purfling strips are inlaid and trimmed flush **21**, an additional trench is cut between the two central strips **22**. Rout this channel precisely to accommodate the pieces of AbLam **23**. The aim should be to set the pieces as flush to the surface as possible **24** to prevent too much loss of color when you sand the shell flush **25**.

Cutting out the soundhole

Whichever style of rosette you have decided on, the final stage involves cutting out the soundhole **26**. Replace the panel pin in the center of the circle and reset the rosette-cutting jig. The soundhole should be cut in two or

Kinkade Tip

AbLam does not always have consistent depth of color as it is a laminate material. Therefore it is best to inlay as flush to the surface as possible, to avoid sanding through the top layer which may reveal something less attractive underneath.

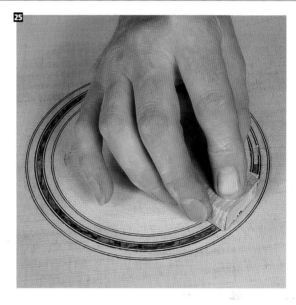

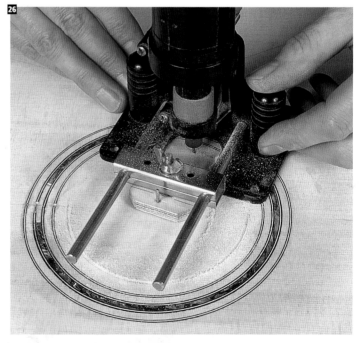

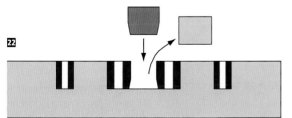

three passes, cutting only to a depth of ½₂ in (1mm) on each pass. This ensures the cleanest possible cut with the least risk of tearout or splintering.

Cutting out the soundboard

From the waste spruce at the bottom of the soundboard cut a ⅝ in (16mm) wide strip—its grain running across, rather than up and down the wood— and put this to one side for use as the reinforcing strip for the back. The other offcuts are saved for bracing patches. Then cut out the soundboard using a band saw with a very fine blade. In the absence of a band saw, a coping saw or even a fret saw will do perfectly well. The soundboard is glued to the

sides oversize, then trimmed, so stay ³⁄₁₆ in (5mm) outside the pencil line as you cut **27**. Work carefully, keeping the blade under control and supporting the soundboard so that it doesn't split.

Feathering the edges

A high-quality, close-grained spruce top will benefit from having its edges feathered: this makes the soundboard more flexible and increases its bass resonance. Use a block plane to reduce the board's thickness around its edges to between ³⁄₂ and ⁷⁄₆₄ in (2.5 and 2.8mm) **28**, taking care to avoid chip-outs. This extra thicknessing procedure can also be achieved by vigorous sanding and scraping during the final

sanding stage, all the time tapping and listening as the wood's tone changes. The feathering process can be omitted with more flexible, lower-grade soundboards, as they are flexible enough due to their quality.

BRACING/STRUTTING

The following instructions describe the method I use to create a slightly domed surface on the soundboard, using curved braces and clamping these against a concave dish in a go-bar press (see page 56). If this process seems too daunting, you could also glue straight braces onto the soundboard while it is clamped against a flat workboard with conventional clamps.

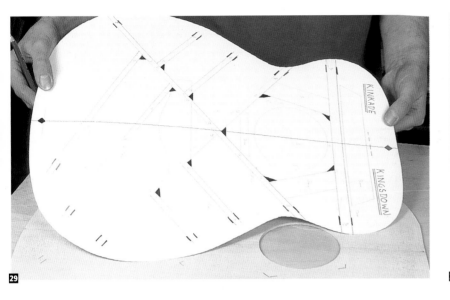

29

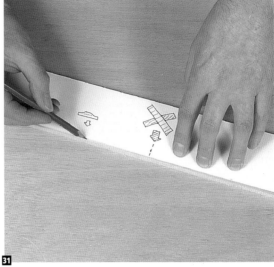

31

Marking the position of the braces

Referring to your plans, make a tracing of the guitar body outline, and mark the extremities and intersections of the braces onto a cardboard template **29**. Then use a soft pencil to transfer these marks onto the inside surface of the soundboard.

Preparing oversize brace blanks

The braces, or struts, are made from split, straight-grained, quarter-sawn Sitka spruce **30**. For maximum stiffness the end grain should be vertical. Cut the pieces ½ in (12mm) longer at each end than shown on the plans, and at least ⁵⁄₁₆ in (3mm) higher. Brace C, for example, is cut to a length of 12 in (300mm) and a height of 1 in (25mm), although the finished dimensions will be 11 in (276mm) long and ¹³⁄₁₆ in (21mm) tall.

Curving the braces

Use a curve template (see page 55) and a 3H pencil to transfer the curves from your templates onto all the braces **31**.

Clamp a brace to the workbench with a spacer underneath. Use a block plane on its side to shape the curve **32**. Repeat the procedure for each of the braces. If you are following my plans, you will need to drill a hole in the C brace, to facilitate access for the trussrod adjustment. This hole is ⅜ in (10mm) in diameter with its center ⁹⁄₃₂ in (7mm) from the gluing surface. Use a brad-point drill bit against a backing piece of wood, to prevent chipout on the bottom surface of the brace.

30

A

B

C

D

E

F

G

L R

32

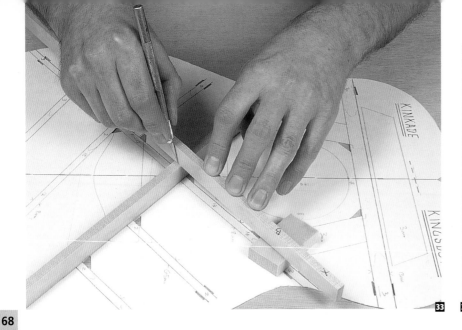

33 **34**

Referring to the plans, dress away the ends of the braces as shown in a gentle curve, starting approximately 1½ in (40mm) in from each end, so as to help identify the gluing surface.

Cutting an X-brace halved joint

Braces A and B intersect in a halved joint to make an X-brace. Lay brace A on the plans, with brace B on top, to determine the angle of crossover. Take a sharp knife and scribe the intersection marks onto brace A, the lower strut **33**. Cut the joint to half the depth of the strut with a modelmaker's back saw **34**.

Position both struts on the plans again, and this time scribe the intersection marks on brace B. Cut the opposite half of the joint and check for fit **35**. The joint must be cut precisely for a snug fit: practice making it on some offcuts until you feel confident of your ability to tackle the real thing.

It is important to note that the X-brace does not form a 90-degree angle, and that the struts can fit together in both "right" and "wrong" ways. The latter dramatically changes the angle, so mark each brace to avoid confusion.

Cutting housings

I like to cut housings in the arms of the X-brace where braces D, E, F, and G butt up against them. This adds strength, it acts as insurance against the braces coming loose should the instrument suffer a knock, and aids the efficient transfer of vibrations, creating a stronger tone. Cut the housings using a small chisel, and shape the brace ends to fit them **36**.

Making the patches and bridge plate

We now turn to the soundboard offcuts saved earlier, from which we will make

35 **36**

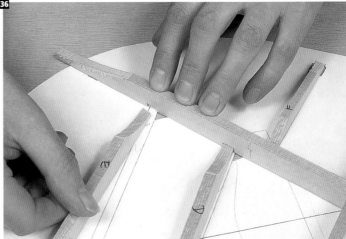

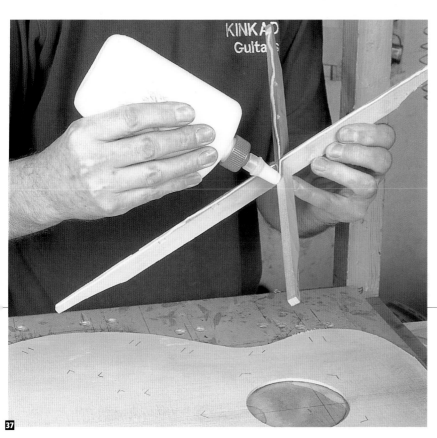

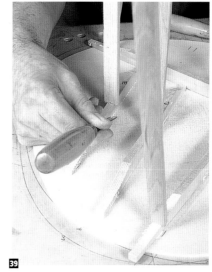

bracing patches. Cut these to the dimensions given in the plans and bevel their edges. Ensure the grain is running up and down as straight as possible.

The bridge plate reinforces the soundboard directly underneath the bridge, at the point at which maximum tension is exerted on the structure by the strings. I use a piece of straight-grain maple about ⁹⁄₆₄ in (3.5mm) thick. Cut to size and bevel the edges. The plate is not meant to fit snugly between the braces: there should be a gap of about ¹⁄₃₂ in (1mm) between them. Leave these parts to settle overnight.

Gluing the braces

Glue the X-brace together with AR glue. Ensure that the bottom surfaces are flush and remedy if necessary. Glue the braces onto the soundboard in

alphabetical order; for example, A and B braces are glued first, then C, and so on. Apply the glue generously to the bottom of the first two braces **37** and lay them on the soundboard, lining them up with the pencil marks. Use the go-bar press to clamp them down **38**, making sure they don't slide out of position before the glue starts to grab. If necessary, apply an extra go-bar to exert additional pressure. Glue squeeze-out is evidence of a close fit: Scrape it off with a chisel as you proceed with each brace **39**. Pay special attention to brace C to ensure that it does not slide sideways. Also make sure that the center line of the trussrod adjustment hole in brace C is lined up with the center line of the guitar. Continue with braces D, E, F, and G.

Apply glue to the patches and position them on the soundboard, using a clamping caul to distribute the pressure evenly. Note that the bridge plate is not applied at this stage. Check that no braces have moved sideways, and make one last inspection to verify that all elements are seated correctly **40**. Leave to dry for two hours.

The X-brace is strengthened at its junction with a capping piece made from an offcut of spruce. Cut a piece of strut measuring approximately 2 in (50mm) long by ⅜ in (10mm) high. Trim the X-brace to finished height with a block plane, then glue the capping piece over the junction of the X-brace.

Gluing the bridge plate

Apply glue to the bridge plate and glue it to the soundboard with a G-clamp through the soundhole, using a caul to spread the pressure, with the top of the soundboard resting on a workboard **41**.

Scalloping the braces

Next comes one of the most exciting stages, where you carve the oversized and rough-shaped braces into their finished form, following the plans. Before you begin, tap the soundboard and listen to the tone. Keep tapping as you carve the braces ever more finely, and you will hear the tone drop as the soundboard becomes looser and more receptive to vibration.

Rest the soundboard on a piece of 1 in (25mm) foam to support and protect its top. Using a 1 in (25mm) bevel-edged chisel, pare away the sides of the braces into a tapered arch cross-section **42**, taking care not to gouge the spruce. It is a good idea to hold the chisel with two hands during the carving process, using one hand as a guide. Continue to tap the soundboard as you work, listening out for the dropping pitch **43**.

It is easy to get carried away with the business of scalloping and voicing the

43

44

guitar. Remember that the voicing can be adjusted when the instrument is finished, by putting your hand through the soundhole and removing more material from the braces with sanding blocks (although it is a bit hard on the forearms!). However, I don't recommend doing this until the guitar is at least a year old and has begun to settle down. A guitar's tone softens over time: I prefer to build mine on the bright side, knowing that they will mellow.

Smoothing the braces

Sand the braces to remove all the chisel marks and leave their surfaces smooth. Start with an 80 grit paper, move to a 150 grit, and finish with 240 grit 44.

The finished soundboard

Congratulations: you are now the proud possessor of one finished soundboard. You have begun your guitar with the biggest challenge, and you have mastered it. Allow yourself some time to appreciate the

achievement. Sit back and admire your work: notice the perfectly jointed top, the smooth curves of the braces, the semigloss sheen of the finely sanded spruce. Give yourself a pat on the back for having produced such a neat and precise piece of craftsmanship 45.

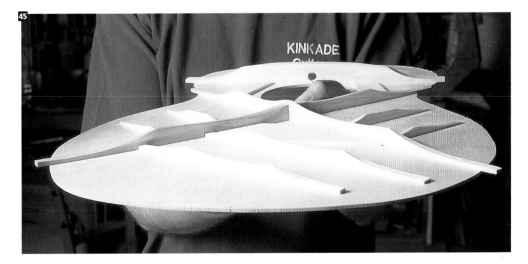

45

Building the Guitar

The Back

- **Jointing**
- **Thicknessing**
- **Bracing/strutting**

The back and sides of the guitar form a resonating chamber in which the vibrations of the soundboard are amplified before being reflected back off the hard surfaces and directed towards the listener. This function calls for a stiff, dense wood, and the back is crafted from a bookmatched, jointed panel of quarter-sawn Indian rosewood, ³⁄₃₂ in (2.5mm) thick. Spruce braces strengthen what is otherwise a relatively flimsy structure.

JOINTING

The two halves of the back are jointed in the same way as the soundboard. Refer back to the previous chapter for detailed instructions, but note the important distinctions that follow, not least the different dimensions.

Preparing the rough boards

Indian rosewood is often obtained rough-cut between ⁵⁄₃₂–¼ in (4–6mm) thick. If you have access to one, run each board through the planer-thicknesser to clean up the surfaces **1**, reducing to no less than ⅛ in (3.5mm) thick. Only top-grade, close-grained woods are suitable for machine planing. Any attempt to machine highly figured material—flame maple, flame koa, or any wood with knots or rising/dipping grain patterns—could seriously damage the wood. If you're using one of these woods, or if you simply don't have access to a planer-thicknesser, then I'm afraid the initial thicknessing has to be done by hand.

Applying glue

When dealing with oily rosewood, I prefer to glue the center joint with a slow-setting epoxy resin. Prior to applying adhesive, clean the gluing surfaces with denatured alcohol or acetone. Apply the epoxy resin to both gluing surfaces before bringing the boards together. Let dry for 24 hours.

The jointing sequence

The jointing sequence runs as follows:

- Prepare the boards.
- Choose the jointing edge.
- Make the center join on the shooting board using a freshly honed plane.
- Check that you have a perfect joint with no light gaps, and remedy if this is not the case.
- Set up the workboard as a baton-and-nail press.

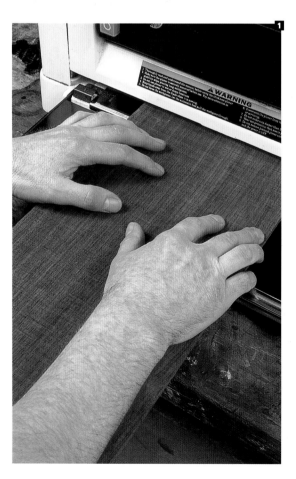

- Apply the relevant glue.
- Clamp up and leave to dry.

THICKNESSING

The back is now reduced to its final thickness, our aim being to finish with a smoothly sanded and scraped surface $\frac{3}{32}$ in (2.5mm) thick. The process is similar to that used for the soundboard, but once again with some important differences to note.

Hand planing

Planing hardwoods, such as rosewood, requires considerable physical effort **2**.

Kinkade Tip

As an alternative to marking the outline of the guitar using the method described, you can also use a transparent template.

There is also a high risk of splintering or chipouts, especially with highly figured woods. Using a toothed blade in the plane can help prevent this.

Machine sanding

Start with 60 grit paper in the power sander and finish with 80 grit **3**. Note that the oil in the rosewood will cause the abrasive surface to gum up more rapidly than usual.

Checking thickness

Monitor the reducing thickness of the back regularly using dial-gauge calipers. When you reach $\frac{1}{8}$ in (3mm), inspect both sides to identify the most attractive surface: this will be the outside of the instrument. Make further reductions on the inside surface to $\frac{7}{64}$ in (2.7mm). Finally, use a cabinet scraper and sanding blocks to make the final reduction to $\frac{3}{32}$ in (2.5mm) and create a smooth outside surface.

BRACING/STRUTTING

The following instructions describe the method I use to create a slightly domed back, using curved braces clamped and glued against a concave dish in a go-bar press, and also a simpler alternative using regular clamping cauls.

Marking the outline of the guitar

Mark the center line on both sides of the back using an HB pencil. Here again you might have difficulty spotting it if your joint was true. Look for the telltale trace of glue on the endgrain. Carefully place your mold (see pages 48–50) on the outside surface of the back. Using the mold as a window, choose the area that reveals the best grain pattern and the least number of flaws. Trace around the inside of the mold with a white pencil (that shows up better on dark woods) to transfer the outline of the guitar onto the back piece **4**.

5

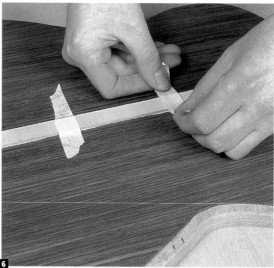

6

Cutting out the back

Cut out the shape of the guitar using a band saw with a very fine blade **5**. Cut ³⁄₁₆ in (5mm) outside the white line—the back is glued to the sides oversize, then trimmed. In the absence of a bandsaw, a coping saw or a fret saw will do perfectly well. Work very carefully, controlling the blade and supporting the back as you cut, to avoid any risk of splitting the wood.

Back reinforcing strip

Now retrieve the ⁵⁄₈ in (16mm) wide perpendicular strip that was cut earlier from the soundboard (see page 66). This is glued to the inside surface of the guitar back to reinforce the butt joint. Referring back to the plans, cut the strip overlength by ⅛ in (3mm) at each end. Ensure the gluing surface is both

clean and smooth and apply a thin film of AR glue to the strip. Secure it in place along the center line with masking tape **6** and use two clamps and a clamping bar to apply pressure evenly along its length. Leave to dry for an hour, unclamp, and clean away the glue squeeze-out while it is still soft.

With the back firmly clamped to the workboard, use a finely set block plane to give a gently arched cross-section to the reinforcing strip **7**. Smooth with sanding blocks.

Marking the position of the braces

Referring to your plans, mark the position of the ends of the braces on the inside of the back.

Preparing oversize brace blanks

The braces are made from the same split, straight-grained, quarter-sawn Sitka spruce with vertical end grain used for the soundboard struts. Cut the pieces ½ in (12mm) longer at each end than shown on the plans, and at least ⅛ in (3mm) higher, but to their finished width. The first brace, for example, is cut 12 in (300mm) long by ¹³⁄₁₆ in (20mm) tall by ⁵⁄₁₆ in (8mm) wide, although its finished dimensions will be 11 in (276mm) long by ⅝ in (17mm) tall by ⁵⁄₁₆ in (8mm) wide.

7

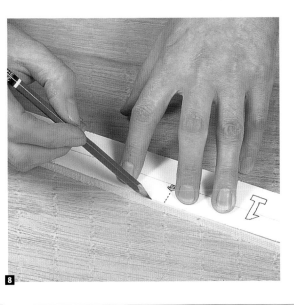

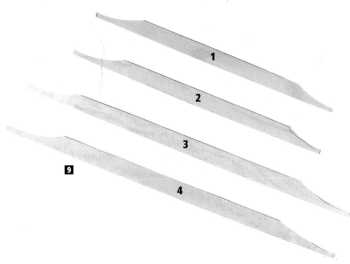

Curving the braces

Use a curve template (see page 55) and a 3H pencil to transfer the curves from the plans to the braces . Clamp a brace to the workbench with a spacer underneath. Use a block plane on its side to shape the curve. Repeat the procedure for each brace. Dress away the ends of the braces in a gentle curve, starting approximately 1½ in (40mm) in from each end **9**. This will help to identify the gluing surface.

Cutting slots in the reinforcing strip

Slots are cut in the reinforcing strip to allow each brace to seat fully as it crosses the center joint. Clamp the brace in position and, using it as a width guide, mark the reinforcing strip on either side with a fine blade **10**. Carefully remove that portion of the strip with a chisel **11**. Work undersize to begin with and expand until you achieve a perfect fit—this keeps the brace stable during gluing.

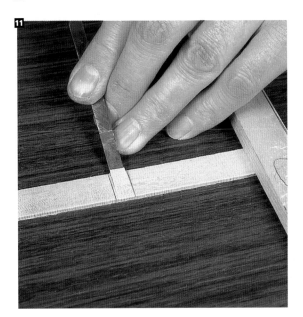

excess glue with a chisel as you go. Leave the braces to dry for two to three hours.

If making a go-bar press seems too daunting, equally good results can be achieved using four separate clamping cauls that match the curvature of the braces . Do not glue more than two braces at once, as the weight of the clamps can easily damage such a light structure.

Whichever method you use, you will enjoy observing the fine arch you have created once the glue has dried.

Gluing the braces

In the go-bar press method 12, the back braces are glued into place individually. Apply glue generously to the jointing side of a brace and position it on the back, lining it up with the pencil marks. Use the go-bar press to clamp it down, making sure it doesn't slide until the initial grab of the glue takes place. If necessary, apply an extra go-bar to exert additional pressure: glue squeeze-out evidences a close fit. Clean up the

Shaping the braces

Rest the back on a piece of 1 in (25mm) foam to support and protect its underside. Referring to the dimensions on the plans, use a block plane to carve the braces to the required height and give them a tapered, arched profile. Safeguard the center strip from inadvertent plane damage by using a protective caul made from a piece of card with a slot cut in the middle **14**.

Smoothing the braces

Starting with coarse sandpaper (80 grit) sand the braces until all surfaces are smooth. Move to a finer 150 grit, and polish to a finish with 240 grit **15**.

Scalloping the ends

Referring to your plans, scallop the ends of the braces with a chisel **16**, and sand smooth.

Finished back

The back is now finished **17**: from two flimsy pieces of hardwood you have created a highly engineered structure that will form the backbone of your guitar. Enjoy a moment of quiet contemplation before the next stage.

Kinkade Tip

During the sanding process, I protect the center reinforcing strip with low-tack masking tape. You can make ordinary masking tape low tack by taping the adhesive side on your clothes. This reduces its strength and will stop it tearing the wood on removal.

The Sides

■ **Preparation and bending**

■ **Top and bottom blocks**

■ **Kerfings and side struts**

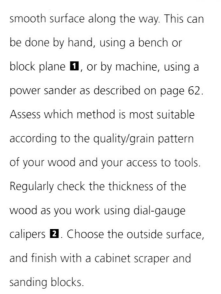

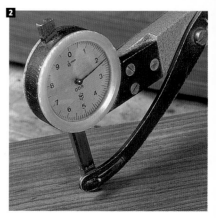

The sides consist of two bookmatched panels of quarter-sawn Indian rosewood about ⁵⁄₆₄ in (2mm) thick. They are bent to the desired shape and then joined with a block at the neck end and at the bottom. Lining blocks, or kerfings, are glued to their edges, for reinforcement and to increase the gluing surface for the attachment of the soundboard and the back. The sides are further reinforced by glueing small struts at intervals across the grain, as a precaution against damage.

PREPARATION AND BENDING

Bending the sides of a guitar is a daunting prospect, even for the most experienced maker. For the beginner, it presents yet another major challenge. But don't panic: all will be explained.

Preparing the rough boards

Start with two slices of oversize quarter-sawn Indian rosewood, about ⁵⁄₃₂ in (4mm) thick. We will first reduce these to ⁵⁄₆₄ in (2mm) thick, giving them a smooth surface along the way. This can be done by hand, using a bench or block plane **1**, or by machine, using a power sander as described on page 62. Assess which method is most suitable according to the quality/grain pattern of your wood and your access to tools. Regularly check the thickness of the wood as you work using dial-gauge calipers **2**. Choose the outside surface, and finish with a cabinet scraper and sanding blocks.

Inspecting the grain pattern

Consider the orientation of the grain and choose the best way to organize the pattern for aesthetic balance, bearing in mind that the sides will taper on their back edge. It is important to mark them on their outsides, remembering that each side is a mirror image of the other. This means that you will have to bend a left side and a right side rather than two of the same. Mark both the boards on the edge that will join the soundboard **3**.

5

4

Kinkade Tip

Bending wood is not an exact science. Some woods do not need soaking in hot water and only require the use of damp rags to provide the moisture. Trial and error is the best guide to how to proceed, although I always bend rosewood wet.

6

Trimming the edges

Mark the width of each side to 3¹⁵⁄₁₆ in (100mm) and trim the edges on a band saw, just outside the line **4**. Lay the sides on the shooting board, one on top of the other, and plane back to the line. At this stage the sides are still overlength. Mark the point at which the waist will occur, leaving an equal portion overlength at each end.

Bending the sides

The principle involved in bending the sides is that when heat is applied to wet wood it can be bent without cracking. The heat, or strictly speaking the steam, softens the fibers, making the wood flexible and allowing you to move it into your chosen curve. As the temperature drops and the wood dries, the new shape is retained. In practice, the process involves using water-saturated timber held against a heated metal former known as a bending iron. Damp rags, positioned between the timber and the iron, help to increase the moisture levels, while a bending strap of thin, flexible metal, supporting the timber on the outside of the curve, serves to increase the temperature.

Care must be taken when applying heat: too much will scorch the wood, especially when dry. While a small amount of scorching on rosewood and other dark timbers can be scraped away, light woods are more of a problem: the marks penetrate deeply and are harder to remove. Guard against scorching by keeping the wood moving; this also helps you avoid creating uneven bends.

Allow the bending iron to heat up fully before you begin: it is ready to use when droplets of water bounce off with a loud sizzle. Soak the rosewood for 15 minutes in a trough of hot water **5**. Work with the bending strap and a damp cloth on the waist portion of the side first, against the flattest part of the iron. A lot of steam is expelled at this stage. Work the wood up and down, heating a couple of inches either side of the waist, gradually concentrating on the tightest part of the curve. As the temperature increases, you'll feel the wood beginning to give and you can apply pressure to create the curve **6**.

7

8

Now move the wood onto the sharper curve of the iron to create the tight shape at the waist. Discard the damp rag and the bending strap. Using two small batons of softwood to support the side, continue this process until the wood is dry, and follows the curvature of the waist as closely as possible. Refer to the mold to check the contour, and repeat the wetting and bending process until you have achieved an accurate match **7**. Remove the wood from the iron and waft it around to reduce the temperature and set the curve.

Work on the upper **8** and lower bouts **9** following the same sequence, beginning with a damp rag and bending strap, then finishing the shape with batons. These curves are much easier to form because they are a lot less extreme. Continue to shape and adjust the curve of the sides until they fit accurately into the mold **10**.

Fitting waist expanders

The bent sides are now left in position in the mold to allow the wood to settle fully into its new shape. They are held in position by waist expanders, made from two appropriate lengths of timber, beveled at the ends to match the curvature of the sides. These are placed across the inside of the mold on either side of the waist and tied together in such a way as to hold the sides firmly in position against the walls of the mold

9

10

Diagram labels: 92° | Side | 92° | 3⅜ in (85mm) | top block | bottom block | 3¹⁵⁄₁₆ in (100mm) | 100° | ⁹⁄₁₆ in (15mm) | side taper | 92°

13

(see fig. 18 on page 83). Keep checking each side for movement during settlement, and rework as necessary. Leave the sides in the mold overnight.

Trimming the sides to length

Both sides are still overlength at both the top and bottom ends, and must be trimmed to size. With the sides in the mold, mark the position of the center line with a knife. Remove the sides, use a set square to score a perpendicular

line from that mark, and cut to length with a gents saw 11. Repeat at the other end. Tape the sides together on the outsides and return the assembly to the mold. The tape serves as a glue barrier for the next process.

TOP AND BOTTOM BLOCKS

The top and bottom blocks are made from mahogany because it has the same coefficient of expansion as the neck, which is also of mahogany. Make sure that the grain of each block runs in the same direction as that of the sides, so that neck, sides, and blocks move in unison during changes in humidity.

Preparing the blocks

With the sides in the mold, use a cabinet scraper to clean the inside surfaces. Any dirt deposited during the bending process could hinder perfect adhesion. Referring to the plans, cut two overlength mahogany blocks, and shape their gluing surfaces to match the curvature of the sides 12. Note that

12

the bottom and top blocks are cut to different heights, because the ⁹⁄₁₆ in (15mm) taper of the sides needs to be taken into account. To cope with the domed shape of the soundboard and back, the block ends are not square 13, but angled as shown with a block plane. Once the angles have been made, the blocks may be cut to their final height of 3¹⁵⁄₁₆ in (100mm) for the bottom block and 3⅜ in (85mm) for the top block. Shape the beveled edges on the blocks with the band saw 14. Finish by smoothing with a sanding block.

14

15

Kinkade Tip

To avoid snapping the kerfings you can wet them, to make them more flexible, or score the kerfs with a knife blade. Support the tight curve at the waist with a strip of cardboard.

Gluing and clamping

Use AR glue to secure the top and bottom blocks in place. Glue the top block so that its top edge is flush with the front edge of the sides. The ⁹⁄₁₆ in (15mm) of side left overhanging will be trimmed off later. Use two clamps for each block, with a caul to prevent denting **15**. Clean up the glue squeeze-out and leave overnight to dry.

KERFINGS AND SIDE STRUTS

Kerfings have been made in a variety of styles over the years, and from different woods. Some classical makers choose not to kerf the lining blocks, but to pre-

bend them to shape before fitting. Ours are made from ⁷⁄₃₂ x ⅝ in (5.5 x 17 mm) rectangular-section strips of mahogany, and we'll need two 34 in (864mm) lengths to do the front and back.

Preparing the kerfings

Plane a bevel on the longer edge of one strip, and repeat on the other. The two strips may now be ganged together with a piece of tape so that the series of saw cuts, or kerfs, that makes the strip of material flexible may be cut together. This can be done with a radial-arm saw or by hand, using a small miter box and gents saw **16**. The miter box is designed so that the saw cuts only to a specific depth.

Gluing the front kerfings

Position the sides assembly in the mold, waist expanders in place, and with the front edge protruding from the mold by about 1 in (25mm). The kerfing strips are easier to manage in approximately 6 in (150mm) lengths than in one piece. Glue them in place, taper side down

and with their flat edge ¹⁄₃₂ in (1mm) proud of the sides, and clamp with strong domestic clothes pins **17**. Clean the glue squeeze-out and leave to dry for two hours. Trim the proud kerfings with a block plane so that they are almost flush.

Creating the side taper

Remove the sides assembly from the mold, insert the stop blocks (see pages 50–51), and replace the assembly the other way up, so that the back edge is now protruding from the mold by about 1¼ in (30mm) with the front edge bearing on the stop blocks to resist downward pressure. Reposition

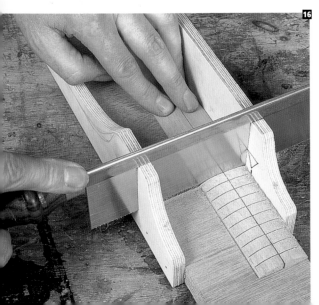

16

17

the waist expander. If you have made a side-tapering jig (see pages 51–52), lay it on the mold and carefully trim the sides using a block plane until they match the depth of the top block **18**. If not, this can be done by eye without a jig, but remember that the taper follows a curve rather than a straight line **19**.

Gluing the back kerfings

The back kerfings are glued in the same way, except that they need to be attached in 3 in (75mm) segments to cope with the geometry of the taper. Work from the top block and ensure that they are neatly clamped all the way round **20**. This kerfing edge is visible

through the soundhole, so make a tidy job of it! Clean up the excess glue and leave to dry. Trim the proud kerfings almost flush with a block plane.

Fixing the side struts

The six side struts are made of Sitka spruce. Cut them to length, then glue with gel superglue and clamp in place, at equal intervals **21**. Clean the glue squeeze-out and shape the ends with a chisel before sanding smooth.

The finished sides

Remove the structure from the mold and observe that this is a remarkable piece of sculpture in its own right **22**.

Curved taper

3¹⁵⁄₁₆ in
(100mm)

Assembling the Body

■ **Fitting the soundboard**

■ **Fitting the back**

Attaching the soundboard and the back to the sides is a delicate operation with two important factors to consider. First, the soundboard and back are both slightly arched structures; this means that the gluing surfaces of the kerfings and the blocks need to be shaped accurately to match them. The angles are more than 90 degrees, and can be finessed with a block plane and/or sanding sticks. Second, the soundboard and back have overlength struts that must be trimmed to fit the housings created in the kerfings.

FITTING THE SOUNDBOARD

Before you begin this process, make accurate notes of your work's key dimensions so far, for future reference. Taking a few photographs will also serve as a useful *aide-mémoire*.

Positioning the sides

You now need to drill a series of holes in the lower half of the mold to accommodate another set of stop blocks. These are positioned to conform to the tapering back edge of the sides, supporting the assembly so its soundboard edge protrudes about ¾ in (19mm) proud of the mold's surface. As an alternative to my method of using dowel stop blocks, small blocks of wood can be nailed to the sides of the mold. Reposition the waist expanders.

Positioning the soundboard

Position the soundboard accurately on the sides, aligning the center lines and datum point at the neck end. Hold in place with masking tape and an elastic strap **1**. Mark the sides and the braces

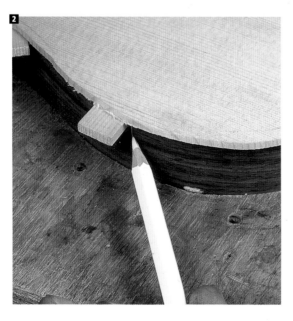

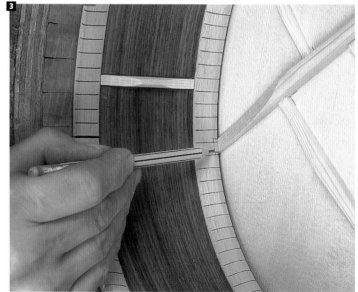

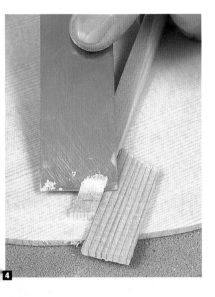

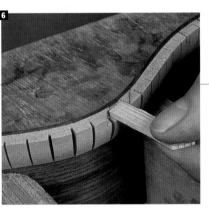

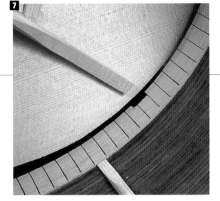

where the two intersect **2** and also where the brace meets the kerfing on the inside **3**. Using these marks, trim the brace ends to their correct length, and chisel to the correct height, using an offcut of soundboard spruce as a depth gauge **4**. Cut the housings in the kerfings with a chisel, using a block of wood to support the sides **5**. Use your gauge again to check the depth **6**. Reposition the soundboard on the sides and check that all parts mate accurately **7**. Remedy as necessary. Do a dry run with the clamping caul.

Gluing the soundboard

Apply AR glue evenly to the surface of the kerfings and blocks. Position the soundboard **8** and apply pressure by screwing down the clamping caul **9**. Inspect inside the body for correct fitting. Clean up any excess glue **10** and leave to dry for at least two hours. Take note of the amount of glue used, and how much squeeze-out this occasioned: you will need to be more

accurate with your use of glue when you are fixing the back, as excess glue is difficult to remove from the inside of the guitar, where it will be visible.

When dry, remove the caul and trim back the overhang of the soundboard using a chisel , or a router with a flush-cutting bit.

Checking the soundboard

Test the flexibility of the soundboard by applying gentle pressure from the outside . You can also tap and listen at this stage. An experienced luthier works intuitively at this point to make decisions concerning the tone of the instrument, removing material from the struts to soften the sound if required. Stand back and admire the internal view of the soundboard attached to the sides 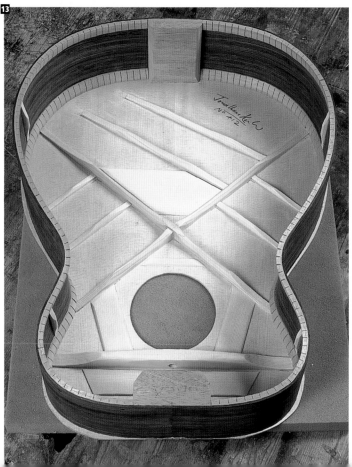. It's your last chance to see it before the back goes on.

FITTING THE BACK

The back is fitted in much the same way as the soundboard, but special attention must be paid to the greater angles at the top block and kerfings.

Repositioning the sides

Refit the assembly in the mold and support with stop blocks so that the back edge is 1¼ in (30mm) proud of the surface at the bottom block position and ⅝ in (15mm) at the top block.

Positioning the back

Mark the strut lengths and the locations of the strut housings on the outside of the body **14**. After ensuring an accurate fit, sand the scalloped ends of the back struts smooth **15**. With the back held in position, mark through the soundhole where the back reinforcing strip meets the top and bottom blocks. Trim to length at both ends **16**. Do a dry run with the clamping caul, and inspect it through the soundhole **17**.

Gluing the back

Apply AR glue to the kerfings and blocks. Don't overdo it—remember the lessons learnt from gluing the soundboard. Clamp up the structure with the caul **18** and leave to dry for three hours. Trim back the overhang with a chisel, or a router with a flush-cutting bit.

Finished body assembly

Remove the completed body from the mold. Marvel at the curvaceous form you have produced. Tap the soundboard and listen to the note produced. Indulge in a moment of fantasy and play some air guitar. You have come a long way.

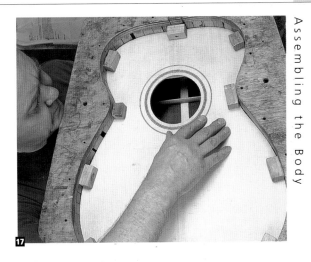

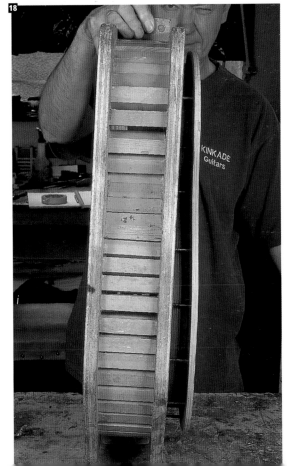

Binding the Body

- ■ **Preparing the front and sides**
- ■ **Cutting the rebates**
- ■ **Creating the bindings**
- ■ **Gluing purflings and bindings**

This chapter demonstrates how to fit a set of holly multiple bindings—a holly banding ¼ x ³⁄₃₂ in (6.5 x 2mm), bordered with black-white-black purflings. The end detail is a holly flash, also bordered with purflings, which are mitered to align with the side purflings. This achieves a decorative effect that displays the skill of the luthier. One downside of the process, however, may be the deterioration of your eyesight!

This pattern can be adapted or simplified to suit. Simply leave out the relevant stages to achieve the desired effect. Whichever design you use, a channel or rebate is cut in the edge to accommodate the chosen materials. All materials are inlaid slightly proud, and are scraped flush after the glue has set.

PREPARING THE FRONT AND SIDES

Place a straight-edge across the sides and look at them in good light **1**. You may notice that the bending process has distorted them, leaving them slightly curved. True up the sides using a large sanding block with 80 grit coarse paper and a cabinet scraper **2**. Work on the sides until they are as even as you can make them. This is most important because any rebating tool will bear on this surface as a guide for its cutting depth.

Sealing the front

Sand the soundboard clean. Mask off the bridge area and seal the remainder of the soundboard with an appropriate medium, relevant to your chosen

3

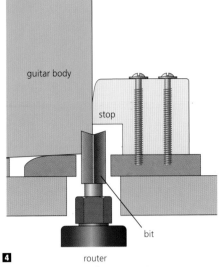

guitar body

stop

bit

4　router

finishing schedule. This keeps the spruce clean, and enables you to achieve a cleaner cut where the rebating tool or router bit cuts into the spruce. It also protects against tearout of the grain when the tape used to hold the bindings in place is removed.

CUTTING THE REBATES

The rebates can be cut by hand using a homemade rebating tool and chisels **3**, but using a router is considerably easier. When setting up a routing jig you must design it to accommodate the fact that the angle made by the sides and the top or back is not 90 degrees—since both the soundboard and back of the instrument are domed, and the sides tapered, this results in angles of over 90 degrees, and in some places over 100 degrees. The rebate must be cut so it is parallel to the plane of the sides, not square to the curvature of the soundboard or back.

I use an inverted router set up from its table by a height of ⅝ in (16mm) **4** and then insert spacers beneath the

instrument to create the correct angles at the cutting position. When cutting the rebates on the soundboard, use a spacer of approximately ½ in (12mm) to cope with its dome of ⅛ in (3mm) **5**. When cutting rebates on the back, use a spacer of approximately ⁷⁄₁₆ in (11mm) for the lower bouts, and remove the

spacer when cutting the rebate at the neck end of the instrument. This accommodates the taper of the sides.

The router bit is tungsten carbide, twin flute, ⅜ in (10mm) in diameter, and has slightly angled blades for a clean cut. By adjusting the depth of the bit and the position of the stop

5

Kinkade Tip

You could save time by fitting plastic bindings that do not have to be pre-bent. Ask your supplier for suitable materials and adhesives.

piece you can create any depth or width of rebate in order to match any custom pattern of bindings **6**.

Adjust the router to create a rebate to fit the dimensions of your binding material. Test on scrap material before routing the rebate on the soundboard and back edges of the body. Make the cut in two or three passes, to reduce the risk of chipping. Check the fit with your binding material **7** **8**.

Reset the router to cut the rebate for the two black-white-black purflings on the edge of the soundboard. The cut should be about two-thirds of the depth of the spruce **9**. Do a preliminary test; proceed slowly to avoid tearout and chips.

Once again, reset the router to cut the rebate for the single black-white-

11

10

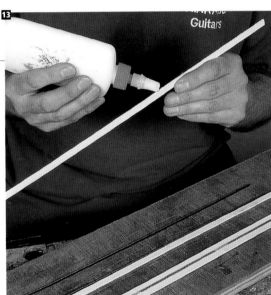

13

14

black purfling on the edge of the back.
Test and again cut carefully **10** **11**.

CREATING THE BINDINGS

In this design, the holly binding strips
are bordered by a purfling strip on the
sides of the guitar **12**. My preference is
to glue the purfling strip to the holly
binding before bending and fitting **13**;
this stops the purflings puckering and
distorting around tight bends, because
they are supported by the binding.

Tape the four purfling-edged
bindings together and mark them
according to their orientation. Use a
bending iron to bend the bindings **14**,

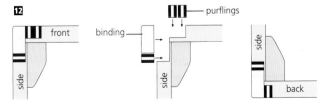

12

front

purflings

binding

side

side

side

back

15

16

following the method used for the sides and using the body as a guide for the curves.

End flash

To create the end flash detail, cut a piece of ³⁄₃₂ in (2.5mm) thick holly to the desired shape. Trace its position with a sharp knife over the join of the sides at the bottom block **15**. Remove the unwanted rosewood with a chisel **16**. Glue the flash in place overlength, with a purfling strip on either side, using AR glue **17**. When dry, trim the ends of the

17

18

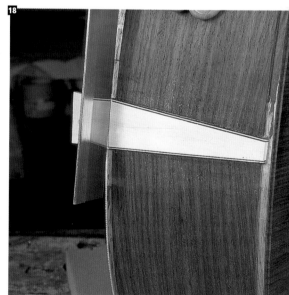

19

flash to the point where they meet the binding **18**. In this design the flash will protrude into the rebate by the width of your purfling strip.

GLUING PURFLINGS
AND BINDINGS

Use AR glue to fix the purflings on the soundboard, starting at the bottom. Secure them in place with masking tape every 2 in (50mm). Check they fit snugly, paying particular attention at the waist. Take care that your fingernails don't mark the soft spruce

at this stage **19**. Prepare the purfling-edged bindings for the soundboard's edge by scraping the gluing surface to remove any dirt left by the bending iron **20**. You can chamfer the gluing surface that meets the side to ensure a close fit. Round off the edge of the bindings that the tape will bear on, as sharp corners can sever the tape.

20

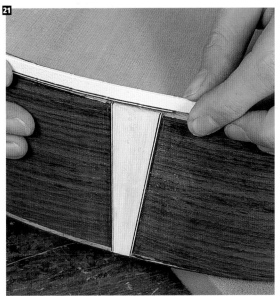

21

The next step is to create the detail where the bindings butt together at the bottom of the body. Locate the bindings at their waist position and secure temporarily with tape. Carefully measure and cut the bindings to length, and then trim and miter the purflings to a close fit with the end flash **21** **22** **23** **24**. Starting at the bottom, glue the bindings onto the soundboard edge, holding them in place with tape **25**.

Repeat this procedure on the back edge, paying particular attention where the bindings butt together at the heel of the instrument, because this joint will be visible **26** **27**. Leave all to dry overnight. This will be the end of a very long day!

Kinkade Tip

Always work with a freshly sharpened scraper. You will probably need to resharpen it several times during this process. Take great care near the soft spruce soundboard!

Scraping back the bindings

Next morning, remove the tape and bring the bindings flush to the instrument. If you are extremely skilled with a block plane you can use it on the soundboard and on the back to remove the bulk of the excess material **28**, before finishing with a scraper. For the less expert, I would recommend using a scraper for the whole process: it's a lot less nerve-racking. Use a scraper also to bring the bindings flush with the sides **29** **30**.

96

The Neck

- **Blocked-up neck construction**
- **Alternative ways of making the neck**

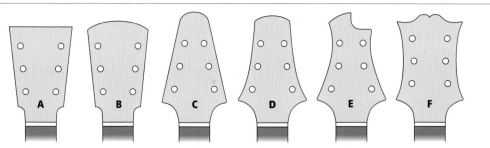

◄ **Headstock alternatives**
Any of the headstock designs illustrated here can be adapted to your own specifications to give an individual style to your guitar. Designs C, D, and E incorporate a taper.

A   B   C   D   E   F

The body of the guitar complete, we now turn our attention to the neck, which anchors the other end of the vibrating strings. There are many ways to construct the neck: I prefer the blocking-up method shown here, but several alternative approaches are discussed at the end of this chapter.

Headstocks, too, come in various shapes and sizes (see figure above), and traditionally incorporate a slight flare. While this design suits certain body shapes, it creates more string friction in the nut, especially on the third and fourth strings, which flare outward toward their machine head at an acute angle. This problem can be overcome by using a tapered or reverse flare design, which allows the strings to run to their tuner in a straight line, or something very near to one.

BLOCKED-UP NECK CONSTRUCTION

This method takes advantage of the fact that is easier—and considerably more economical—to obtain a straight-grained piece of high quality timber in a smaller thickness than would be required if you were to cut the neck from a single block. A standard 40 x 3¼ x 1 in (1020 x 82 x 25mm)

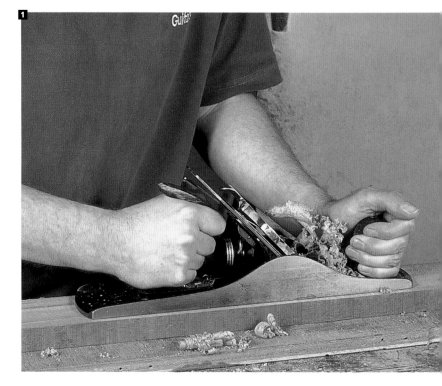

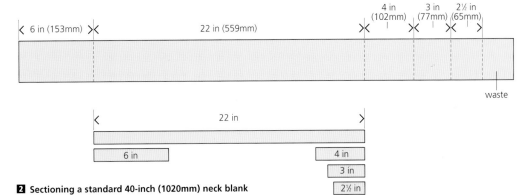

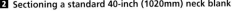

2 Sectioning a standard 40-inch (1020mm) neck blank

blank of quarter-sawn mahogany is cut
into sections. These are glued together
to form a blank, from which the neck is
carved. Assuming the wood is perfectly
quartered, if you keep the orientation
of the grain constant and make flawless
glue joints, the finished neck will
appear to have been cut from a single
piece of timber.

Blocking-up

Plane and scrape smooth both faces of
the mahogany blank **1** and inspect the
grain for straightness. If you plan
carefully, you will be able to lose any
flaws during the marking-out
procedure. Mark the blank into lengths
using the measurements in diagram **2**,
and cut with a band saw **3**. Check
the fit of the gluing surfaces **4** to
ensure they are completely flat.

5

Remedy any unevenness using a block plane and scraper.

Thoroughly clean the work area. Organize your clamps and do a dry run to check the fit. Apply AR glue to the heel pieces and assemble on top of each other, one at a time. Clamp the heel pieces together with the neck resting on its side on the bench, a sheet of paper between the neck and the

bench acting as a glue barrier. The pieces may attempt to slide out of place but with care and correct positioning of the clamps you should be able to hold them in line.

Glue the remaining piece to the headstock end, ensuring you stick it to the correct side **5**. Leave to dry. This process could use most of your clamps, so I usually do it last thing at night.

Cutting out

When dry, square up at least one side of the glued-up neck blank **6**. This enables you to position it on its side on the bed of the band saw, ensuring accurate cuts. Referring to the diagrams **7**, draw a center line; then trace the neck outline on its top surface using a transparent template **8**. Refer to your plans and mark the cutting lines on the

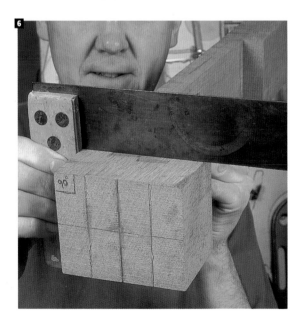

6

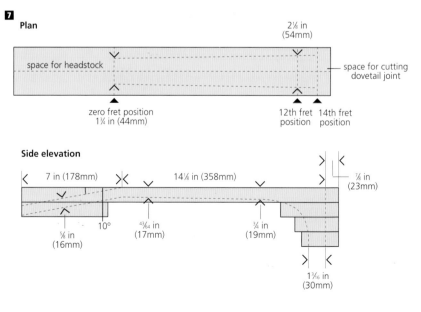

7

Plan

2⅛ in
(54mm)

space for headstock

space for cutting
dovetail joint

zero fret position
1¾ in (44mm)

12th fret
position

14th fret
position

Side elevation

7 in (178mm)

14⅛ in (358mm)

⅞ in
(23mm)

10°

43⁄64 in
(17mm)

¾ in
(19mm)

⅝ in
(16mm)

1³⁄₁₆ in
(30mm)

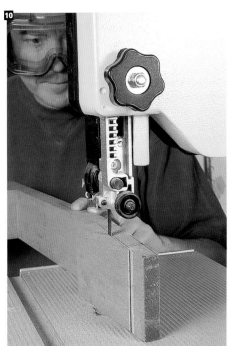

side of the blank . The headstock angle is created by measuring five-and-a-half units along and one unit down. With the neck on its side, cut out the angled headstock on the band saw, cutting just outside the line . Plane the face of the headstock back to the line to leave a smooth surface . Redraw the center line and trace the headstock shape onto this surface 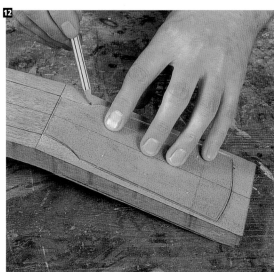.

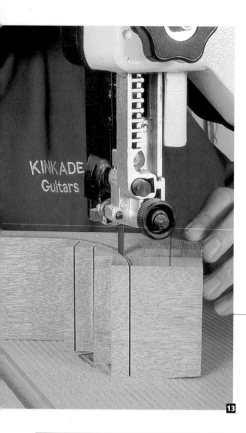

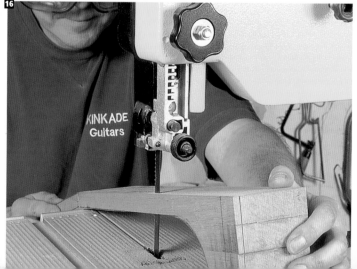

With the neck still on its side, use the band saw to cut the curved line of the heel, and along the back edge of the neck **13**. The depth of the neck has now been reduced **14**. With the blank facing upward, make two small cuts on either side of the neck at the zero fret position, stopping ⅟₁₆ in (1.5mm) short of the marked width of the neck **15**. This makes it easier to remove the waste timber in the next step.

Cut ⅟₁₆ in (1.5mm) outside the line of your neck plan on both sides, starting

17

from the heel and moving toward the headstock **16**. Take care guiding the blade when the heel slides off the bed of the band saw. Now create the headstock shape, cutting outside the line. You have now completed the band saw work **17**. Referring to diagrams **18** (end view) and **19** (bottom view), create the taper on the heel with a chisel **20** and plane to the line **21**.

Rounding off

The neck blank at this stage is slightly oversize and rectangular in cross section. The next task is to begin rounding it off. This is done in stages, because wood has the endearing habit of moving every time material is removed. Stresses are relieved from its structure and as a result it moves out of

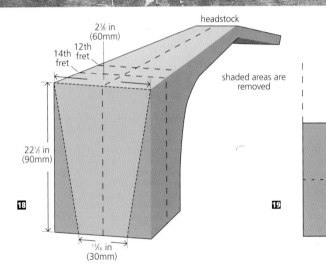

headstock

2⅜ in (60mm)

14th fret
12th fret

shaded areas are removed

22½ in (90mm)

18

1³⁄₁₆ in (30mm)

19

1³⁄₁₆ in (30mm)

1³⁄₁₆ in (30mm)

20

KINKADE Guitars

21

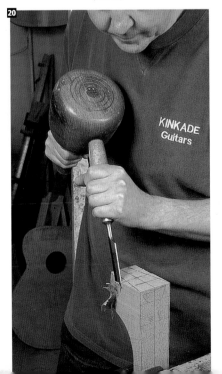

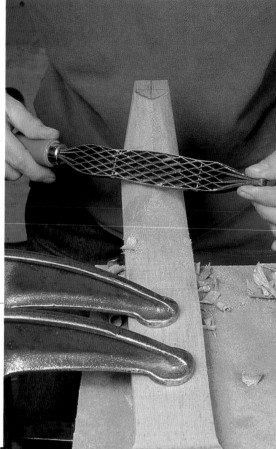

line. Clamp the neck blank firmly to the bench, face down. Starting at the heel, begin to shape a rounded profile. Working carefully, remove the bulk with a chisel **22** and finish off with a rasp **23**. Rotate the blank and round off the neck at the headstock end using a chisel **24**, or use a rasp if you prefer.

Clamp the headstock face down on the bench, with the heel-end of the neck facing toward you. Begin to shape the shaft of the neck into a rounded profile, connecting the two contoured ends. Remove the bulk of the material with a chisel **25** and finish with a spokeshave or rasp **26**. Make sure you don't lose any width from the plan of the fingerboard on the face of the neck blank during the carving process. Once you have joined the contoured ends

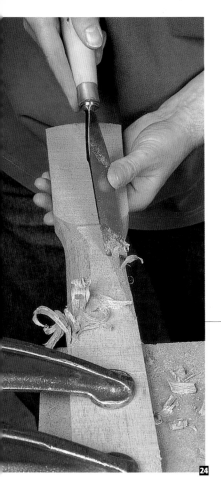

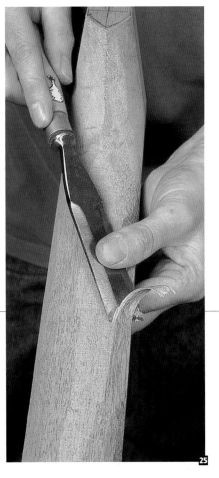

you have a roughed-out neck blank that is oversize by ⅛ in (3mm), ready for the final carve.

It is wise at this stage to leave the neck to settle for a few days, in case any movement occurs: in my experience it always arches back a little. Should this happen, true the face of the neck with a plane prior to fitting it to the body.

ALTERNATIVE WAYS OF MAKING THE NECK

Another method of construction—perhaps the most obvious—involves carving the neck from a solid block. But this is hardly an economical use of wood in these days of scarce resources. It is also difficult to find high quality quarter-sawn wood in the required dimensions. Assuming you had such a

piece, a more efficient move would be to cut two necks nesting opposite one another **27**.

A further alternative is to draw outlines from a template of the neck profile onto a 30 x 5⅝ x 1 in (760 x 140 x 25mm) piece of slab-sawn wood in a nested fashion **28**. Cut the shapes out with a band saw and glue them together, re-orienting the grain pattern to match that of the quarter-sawn wood. This method can be adapted by including thin slices of a contrasting color of wood in between the sections, to create a neck with attractive lines or stripes along it—mahogany with stripes of maple or rosewood works well, or maple with stripes of rosewood or walnut. Both of these produce striking visual results.

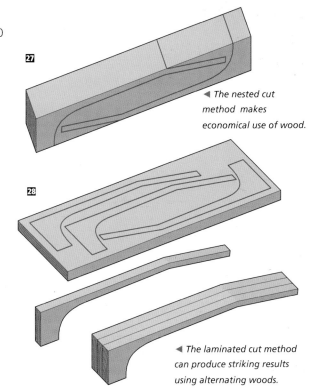

◄ The nested cut method makes economical use of wood.

◄ The laminated cut method can produce striking results using alternating woods.

The Neck-to-Body Joint

- ■ **Neck angle**
- ■ **The routed dovetail joint**
- ■ **The dovetail by hand**
- ■ **Alternative neck-to-body joints**

center line

⁵⁄₆₄–⁷⁄₆₄ in (2–3mm) gap at bridge position

1

2

The neck is joined to the body of the guitar with a classic woodworker's joint of great mechanical strength, the stopped tapered dovetail. Despite its fearsome reputation, this interlocking joint is easier to make than it looks—and enormously satisfying to get right.

NECK ANGLE

The neck does not join the body at 90 degrees: if it did the guitar would be unplayable. Instead the neck is set in such a way that a straight-edge resting on its surface and projecting over the body would arrive at the bridge

position some ⁵⁄₆₄–⁷⁄₆₄ in (2–3mm) above the surface of the soundboard **1**, with the center lines of the neck and body aligned **2**. This is called the neck angle and it is critical because it determines both the string height at the bridge and the playing action—or height of the strings above the fingerboard—of your guitar. A correct neck angle allows the playing action to be adjusted according to preference, and provides space to amend any distortion that might occur over time. To understand the importance of neck angle, imagine your finished guitar with a hinged neck-to-body joint. If the neck were pulled forward toward the soundboard, the action of the strings would become higher. Conversely, if the neck were pitched backward, the strings would eventually lie flat on the fingerboard and the guitar would be unplayable, unless the bridge saddle were raised to an unfeasible height. Our aim is to end up with a gap of around ⅜ in (9.5mm) between the line of the top of the fingerboard and the surface of the

soundboard at the bridge position **3**. Angle A is approximately 88 degrees and Angle B is approximately 92 degrees.

THE ROUTED DOVETAIL JOINT

Start by checking for flatness across the body's sides in the area where the joint housing will be cut **4**—any curvature in this area is fatal—and remedy if

4

5

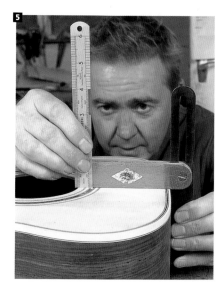

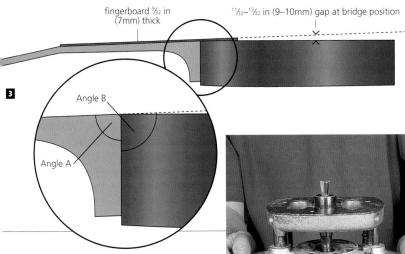

fingerboard ⁹/₃₂ in
(7mm) thick

¹¹/₃₂–¹³/₃₂ in (9–10mm) gap at bridge position

Angle B

Angle A

3

6

7

8

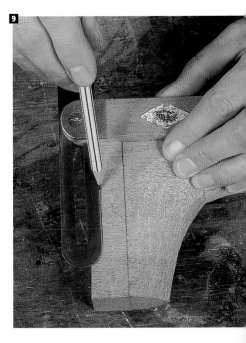

9

necessary. Fasten a ³/₃₂ in (2.5mm)-thick shim of wood at the bridge position with double-sided adhesive tape. Rest a straight-edge on the shim, and observe the angle created at the neck end. Set a sliding bevel to mimic the angle **5**.

I make this joint using a jig that matches the router, set up with its template guide **6**, but some readers will figure that it is quicker to cut a single dovetail joint by hand, and turn to the end of the chapter.

Clamp the guitar into the jig using a caul inside the body **7**. Set the router bit at a fixed depth and, carefully supporting the router's weight, slowly cut the joint housing in the body **8**. Wear protective gear, and use dust extraction on the router.

With the sliding bevel, trace the measured angle onto the end of the neck **9** and trim to match the depth of

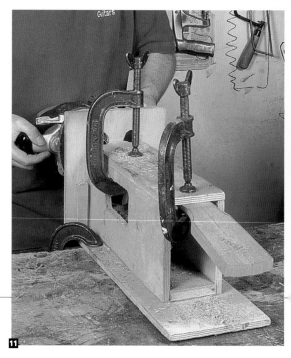

10 **11**

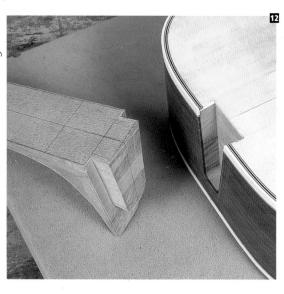

12

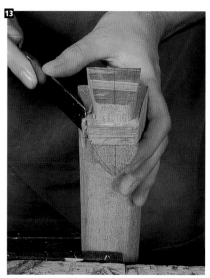

13

14

15

the dovetail. Adjust the neck half of the jig to match that angle **10**. Using the router and the same template guide, cut the dovetail pin in the end of the neck **11**. You have now created a roughed-out dovetail joint **12**.

Fitting the neck and body

Refine the approximate taper you put on the heel in the previous chapter **13**. A concave curve here is both traditional and aesthetically appealing.

To ensure a close fit, pare away the shoulders of the pin so that only its edges touch the body **14**. Assemble the joint dry to assess center line alignment and neck pitch. I design my jig so that the neck is sitting proud of the body at this stage, by approximately ⅜ in (9mm). Using a straight-edge, compare the gap at the bridge position with the amount of neck protruding from the body, and carefully assess the neck pitch **15**.

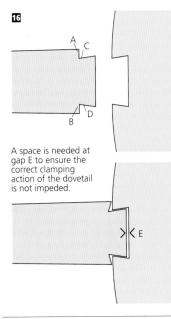

16

A space is needed at gap E to ensure the correct clamping action of the dovetail is not impeded.

17

18

Use a sanding stick to work on shoulders A and B to remedy any misalignment of the neck **16**: removing material from either side will turn the neck in the direction from which material was removed, and relieving wood from the bottom of the heel will create greater pitch. Remember, small adjustments here effect large changes. When you are satisfied that the pitch and alignment are correct, work on surfaces C and D with sanding sticks to allow the neck to fit further into the body **17**, until it is just a fraction proud of the soundboard surface **18**. A good fit here will transmit the strings' vibrational energy efficiently: use chalk to help reveal high spots on the faces.

It is possible, as you finesse the fit, to remove too much material from one side of the dovetail pin, inducing a twist in the neck. If this happens, remedy it by gluing shims of wood to the pin and start the process again.

Use a curved rasp and sandpaper to finish the heel shape **19**. Mark the end of the heel **20** and trim to fit a heelcap. Prepare an oversize heelcap from ⅛ in (3mm) thick holly, ensuring a close fit to the body **21**. Glue the heelcap onto the neck with gel superglue, while the neck is attached to the body, using a polythene caul to isolate the glue **22**.

19

20

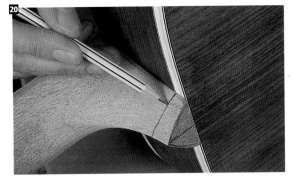

21

22

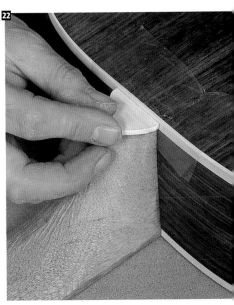

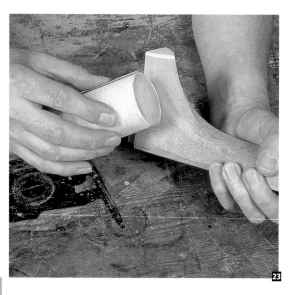

Trim the heelcap and sand flush to the heel **23**. The neck is now ready to be glued to the body **24**. Apply AR glue to both halves of the joint. Assemble and clamp with cauls **25**, cleaning up the glue squeeze-out with damp tissues. The tapered dovetail design has a self-clamping action and usually this is all that is required to hold the joint. Under some circumstances, moisture from the glue may cause the heel of the neck to pull away from the body. If this happens, hold it in place with a sash clamp **26**. Leave to dry overnight.

THE DOVETAIL BY HAND

To make a dovetail joint without a router, first make an acrylic template. Mark lines on the body **27** and neck **28**. Use a small gents saw to cut the housing in the body following the lines. You can only go about halfway, after which you chisel out to the full depth following the saw line. Cut the dovetail pin in the neck, creating the desired angle using the sliding bevel. Then follow the procedure detailed in Fitting the Neck and Body (page 106).

ALTERNATIVE JOINTS

Mortise and tenon

This joint is used on many electric guitars and is a little easier to make. One disadvantage, however, is the lack of a self-clamping action, so more clamps are needed to hold the structure in place while the glue sets.

Dowel and epoxy

Here neck and body are joined with a flush joint. After ensuring you have made the correct angles, arrange two

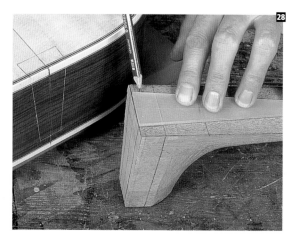

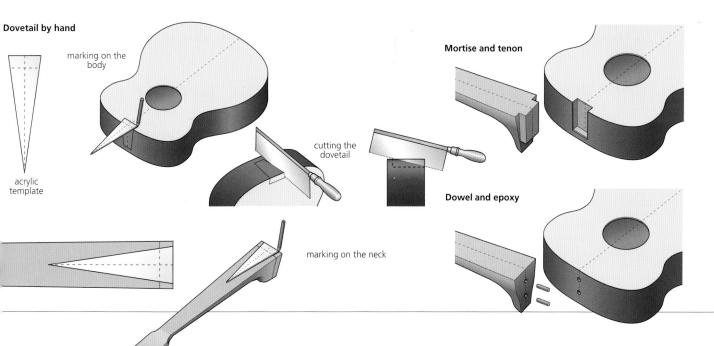

Dovetail by hand

marking on the body

acrylic template

cutting the dovetail

marking on the neck

Mortise and tenon

Dowel and epoxy

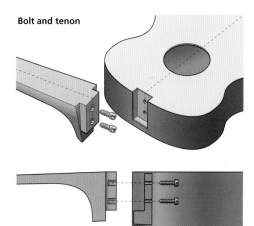

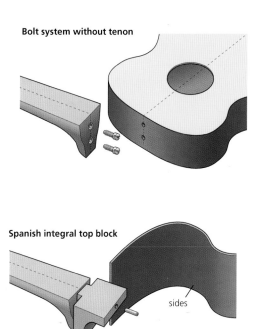

Bolt and tenon

Bolt system without tenon

Spanish integral top block

sides

dowels to hold the joint in place, and fix with epoxy resin. Many makers around the world use this system and claim it is more than strong enough.

Bolt system and tenon

The effects of string tension may cause the soundboard to rise over time, leaving the guitar with an action that is too high. If there is insufficient space for adjustment at the bridge then the problem can only be remedied by re-pitching the neck angle. This relatively simple neck-to-body joint is used by some luthiers in factory production and has the big advantage that it makes neck removal and resetting a relatively easy affair. Two threaded brass inserts are set into a tenon, spreading the stresses over a large area of wood.

An alternative but weaker version of this system is made without a tenon, with the brass inserts set directly into the heel of the instrument.

Spanish integral top block system

This approach does away with the joint altogether, which gives it distinct tonal advantages because glue joints tend to inhibit vibrations. Here the sides of the guitar fit into slots cut at the end of the neck, and the trussrod bears on the neck-extension "block" that supports the fingerboard. This creates a distortion-free zone for the fingerboard because it is supported on the same piece of wood along its length, avoiding any variation in shrinkage between the top block and neck material that is inherent in other methods. The sides, soundboard, and neck are glued together in one speedy operation. The trussrod is adjusted via the soundhole. The only slight drawback is the protruding neck, which makes routing channels for the bindings a little trickier; but it does mean that you don't have to spend half a day making a dovetail joint.

The Trussrod

- **Making the trussrod**
- **Cutting the trench**
- **Installing the trussrod**

Trussrods come in many styles and designs, but all have the same purpose: to reinforce the neck and compensate for its tendency to bow under tension from the strings. I use a compression-style trussrod of my own making, which is very effective when accurately fitted. It is also compact and lightweight, a big advantage since I believe that the less metal inserted in the neck, the better.

The rod is installed so that it can be adjusted through the soundhole; this makes it quite a complicated job, so some readers might feel happier using a ready-made version from a luthier supply company, which will be quicker, and somewhat simpler, to fit.

MAKING THE TRUSSROD

The key elements of the trussrod are shown in the diagram below in (from top to bottom) part-machined, fully machined, and fully assembled stages. When making a trussrod from scratch, the first priority is to source the compression nut, as this will determine the diameter and thread of the trussrod. I prefer a nut with a hexagonal (Allen key) socket.

Referring to the plans, cut a length of mild steel rod, ³⁄₁₆ in (5mm) in diameter, or to suit your nut. Take an appropriate die and cut ⅜ in (10mm) of thread at one end of the rod and ¾ in (20mm) at the other ❶. Prepare the anchor nut from a ⅜ in (10mm) diameter brass rod, drilled ❷ and tapped with a thread to match the rod ❸. Your local tool supplier will be able to advise you on thread dimensions. File a slot across the threaded hole on one side of the anchor nut and screw the opposite end

mild steel rod

anchor nut blank

brass strip

rod with threads cut

tapped and threaded
anchor nut with slot cut

bearing washer with
beveled edges

compression
nut

completed trussrod assembly

▲ **Stages of trussrod construction**

3

4

on to the shorter threaded end of the steel bar so that two threads protrude from the nut. Hammer the end of the rod so that it deforms into the slot, permanently locking the nut in place.

Prepare a bearing washer from a length of ⅛ in (3mm) thick brass strip, and drill a hole large enough for the rod to pass through **4**, beveling the edges to prevent it snagging. Wax the rod along its length **5** and melt a little wax into its threaded end **6** to stop glue clogging the threads during installation. Cover the rod with a thin plastic sleeve to prevent it vibrating.

CUTTING THE TRENCH

Inspect the dovetail joint and fill any gap between the pin and the housing by gluing in a shim of wood, as the rod will compress this area. Check that the surface of the neck is absolutely flush to the surface of the body and if not, remedy with the plane. The trench that houses the trussrod varies in depth—refer to the plans for details—and the plywood jig used **7**, **8** is thicker at the

5

6

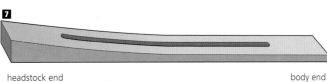

7

headstock end   body end

8

9

10

11

Kinkade Tip

When routing the trench, ensure your routing kit is in top condition. Always use tungsten carbide cutting bits. Worn bits can result in you cutting a slot deeper than planned, as the bit can be dragged out of the chuck.

headstock end, becoming shallower as it curves toward the body. With the router in the jig, carefully cut a trench ¼ in (6mm) wide **9** leaving just ⅛ in (3mm) of neck backing the slot. The positioning is critical: much shallower than this and the compression effect won't work; much deeper, and you risk breaking through the neck. Note that if you change the depth of the neck in your design, you will need to calculate an appropriate depth for the trench.

Making a hole for the anchor piece at the headstock end of the neck is a delicate operation. If the hole is too deep you might uncover it during neck-carving operations later. Start the hole with a brad-point drill bit **10**. Cut to a depth of $^{11}\!/_{32}$ in (9mm). Make sure that you stop before you come out the other side! Carefully increase the depth to $^{7}\!/_{16}$ in (11mm), using a handheld miniature drill fitted with a milling bit **11**.

INSTALLING THE TRUSSROD

Prepare a fillet of maple to fit the width of the trench, shaping its bottom surface to match the curve of the trench. Cut it to length but leave it overheight. Remove the nut and bearing washer from the trussrod and slide it into position from the headstock end in a dry run. Assuming all fits satisfactorily, remove, apply AR glue to the trench, and reposition the trussrod in the slot. Slip the bearing washer and the compression nut onto the end of the rod as it enters the body, before seating the anchor nut at the other end **12**. Apply glue to the maple fillet and clamp it in place **13**. Clean up the glue squeeze-out, remembering to check inside the guitar, and leave to dry. Plane the fillet flush to the surface of the neck **14**. The installation is now complete at both ends **15**, **16**.

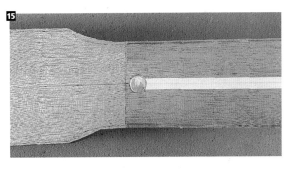

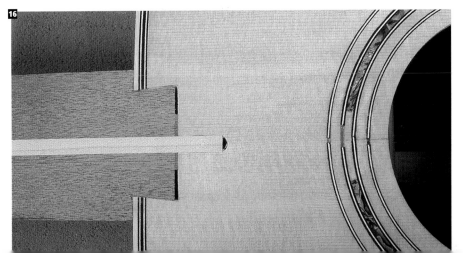

The Fingerboard

■ **Preparing the fingerboard**

■ **Cutting the fret slots**

■ **Trimming and gluing the fingerboard**

The guitar, in common with most stringed instruments today, utilizes what is known as an "equal tempered" scale, a sort of musical compromise in which no interval sounds more unpleasant than its neighbour. This enables the musician to play equally tunefully in any key. The geometrical key to the equal tempered scale is the magic number 17.817, which is used to calculate fret positions, as shown here.

Accuracy is imperative in marking-out and cutting the fret slots if the instrument is ever to play in tune. So take courage, and prepare yourself for another critical stage in the construction of your guitar!

► *The interval between frets is calculated as follows: Divide the desired scale length by 17.817 to give the distance between the nut and the first fret. Subtract that distance from the scale length, and divide this number by 17.817 to get the distance between the first and second fret. Repeat this formula working up the fingerboard to calculate all fret positions for any desired scale length. As a cross-check against possible error, the twelfth fret position should be exactly half that of the scale length.*

► *The chart on the right gives the positions of all the frets, in the form of mean distances from the nut, for the 25.4 in (645.2mm) scale length guitar constructed in this book.*

FRET POSITIONS

Calculation of fret positions for a 25.4 in (645.2mm) scale length:

25.4 ÷ 17.817 = 1.4256047 = distance from nut to 1st fret

25.4 − 1.425 = 23.974396 = remaining length

23.974396 ÷ 17.817 = 1.345591 = distance from 1st to 2nd fret

1.425 + 1.345 = 2.7711957 = distance from nut to 2nd fret (cumulative distance)

Distance from nut	inch	mm
1	1.4256	36.21
2	2.7712	70.39
3	4.0412	102.65
4	5.2400	133.10
5	6.3715	161.85
6	7.4395	188.97
7	8.4475	214.58
8	9.3990	238.75
9	10.2971	261.75
10	11.1447	283.09
11	11.9448	303.42
12	12.7000	322.60
13	13.4128	340.71
14	14.0856	357.80
15	14.7206	373.93
16	15.3200	389.15
17	15.8857	403.52
18	16.4198	417.09
19	16.9238	429.89
20	17.3995	411.97

2

3

4

PREPARING THE FINGERBOARD

Use a plane and scraper to smooth both surfaces of the fingerboard blank, leaving it approximately ⁵⁄₁₆ in (8mm) thick **1**. Using a clear acrylic template to allow you to select the best area of grain pattern, clearly mark out the plan of your fingerboard on the blank **2**. Trim off the excess and plane the edges, leaving the fingerboard ¹⁄₃₂ in (1mm) wider than the planned finished width on each side and also slightly overlength. The edges will be trimmed back to the line only after sawing the fret slots, as this process can lead to chipout at the slot ends.

CUTTING THE FRET SLOTS

The fret slots are cut to match the fret wire you intend to use. In most cases a slot width of approximately 0.023 in (0.6mm) is required: refer to pages 126–131 for more information.

Tape a ruler to the center line of the fingerboard so that the zero position is aligned with that of the fingerboard. Using a fine-bladed craft knife, mark out the positions of the frets **3**. Using a sliding bevel, score the fret positions perpendicular to the center line across the width of the board **4**. Following these lines, cut the fret slots ³⁄₃₂ in (2.5mm) deep using a fretting saw **5**.

Cutting with the aid of a jig

Jigs and templates for varying scale lengths are available from luthier suppliers **6**. Use double-sided adhesive tape to fix the fingerboard to the template, which is indexed along its edges for the desired scale length. Locate the required fret position using a

5

6

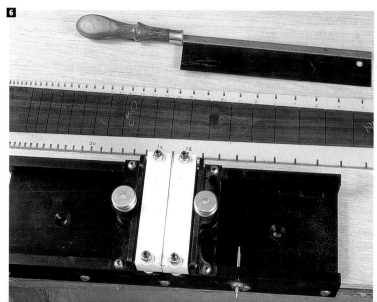

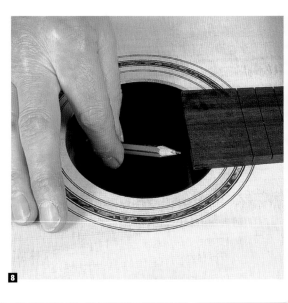

7 **8**

miter box with an indexing pin. Hold the saw firmly in place in a depth-adjustable jig and cut the slots with speed and accuracy.

TRIMMING AND GLUING THE FINGERBOARD

Clamp the fingerboard to the workbench with a spacer underneath. Turn the plane on its side and trim the edges of the fingerboard to the finished width **7**. Position the fingerboard on the guitar and trace the outline of the soundhole on the underside of the

fingerboard **8**. Trim the fingerboard end to the desired profile, cutting from the back to avoid chipping the edges of the gluing surface. Sand smooth. Cut through the fingerboard at the zero fret position **9**. This will be the location of the nut. Sand the edges of the soundhole to a round and smooth profile **10**, as access will be obstructed by the fingerboard after gluing.

Install two small sharpened locating pins in the neck **11**: these will stick into the bottom surface of the fingerboard and prevent it from sliding out of position during the gluing process.

Apply AR glue to the fingerboard **12**, then locate the pin positions and clamp up **13**. The pressure of the clamps is spread with a block, which has a slight convex curve on the surface it presents to the fingerboard. The effect of moisture from the glue creates a reverse bow with a ³⁄₆₄ in (1mm) curve.

The part of the fingerboard being glued to the body has a separate block to accommodate the subtle change in angle between the neck and body. The caul inside the guitar is designed with a portion removed to avoid the trussrod nut **14**. Clean up the glue squeeze-out,

9
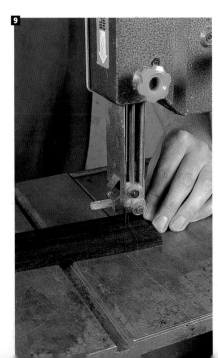

10

11
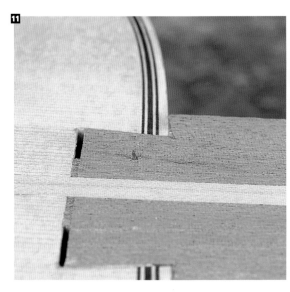

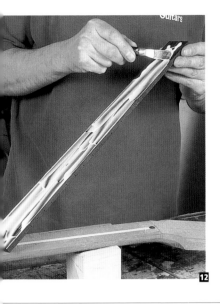

taking extra care on the soundboard area, and leave to dry overnight.

You can now trim the overwide neck flush with the edge of the fingerboard. Work slowly and carefully with a chisel, especially when close to the body **15**. Use a rasp to create a rounded profile on the neck. Reduce the combined neck and fingerboard depth to $^{15}/_{16}$ in (24mm) at the first fret position, and to 1 in (26mm) at the ninth fret position **16**. The neck is still overdepth, but this will be reduced during the fingerboard shaping process, once the parts have had time to settle.

Kinkade Tip

Locating pins can be inserted into holes that are drilled through the fingerboard at appropriate fret positions. The clamping caul must have holes to accommodate them. The pins are removed after the gluing process.

Mold

Soundboard

Back

Sides

Body

Neck

▶ **Fingerboard**

Fretting

Finishing

The Head Veneer

■ **Fitting a head veneer to the headstock**

■ **Drilling holes for the tuning machines**

■ **Creating the nut seating trench**

■ **Inlaying a mother-of-pearl logo**

1

2

3

You need to have bought your tuning machines before embarking on this stage of construction, as these determine the correct headstock depth and hole diameters.

FITTING A HEAD VENEER TO THE HEADSTOCK

Prepare an oversized veneer blank, approximately ³⁄₃₂ in (2.5mm) thick: we show ebony, but you could use any hardwood with an interesting grain pattern. Using the headstock template as your guide, trim the blank to ³⁄₁₆ in (5mm) oversize **1**. Apply AR glue to the headstock face and position the veneer. Clamp with a polythene-covered caul to isolate the glue. Maneuver the clamps in order to prevent sliding, ensuring that the veneer butts up tight against the end of the fingerboard **2**. Leave to dry for a few hours.

Mark a center line on the veneer. Trace around the template and use a block plane and fret saw to trim both

4

5

veneer and headstock back to that line, ensuring that the sides are square to the face **3**, **4**. Use a chisel, plane, or gouge to reduce the depth of the headstock to the appropriate size to suit the tuning machines **5**, **6**.

DRILLING HOLES FOR THE TUNING MACHINES

The holes for the tuning machines used here are drilled in two stages. First drill a hole to accommodate the shaft of the tuning machine. Then expand this with a counterbore on the headstock face to fit the press-fit bushings. For accurate perpendicular drilling into the headstock, prepare a guide from ¾ in (18mm) plywood on a drill press. Clamp the guide to the front of the headstock, with a caul of plywood on the back to reduce chipout. Using a brad-point drill bit diminishes chipout on entry **7**. Expand the holes with a counterbore, to match the depth of the bushings **8**. Offer the machine heads up to check the fit: you may need to ream out the holes a little to prevent binding **9**.

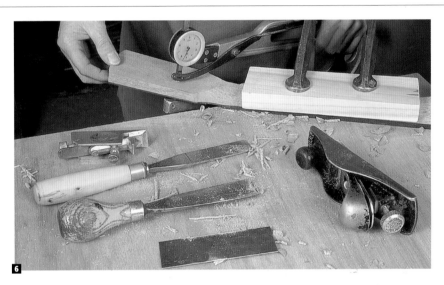

6

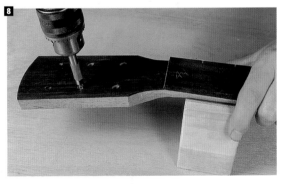

7

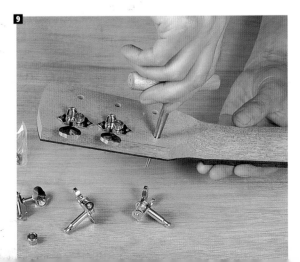

8

9

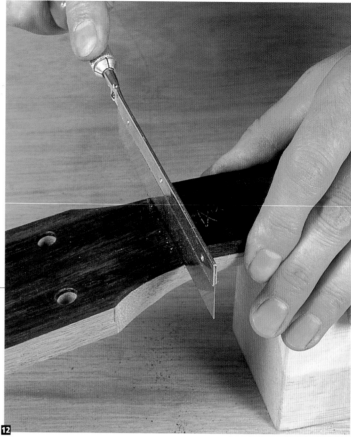

CREATING THE NUT SEATING TRENCH

Take a nut blank measuring 2 x ⅜ x ³⁄₁₆ in (50 x 10 x 5mm) and check its surfaces are flat and square. Use a wide chisel **10**, a craft knife **11**, a model-maker's back saw **12**, and a narrow chisel **13** to make a trench to house the nut **14**. It should butt closely against the end of the fingerboard **15** and be a snug, if not a tight, fit. Avoid chipping the veneer with your chisel when you exit the trench.

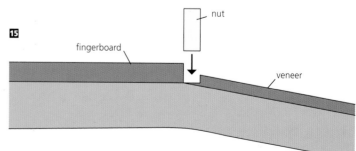

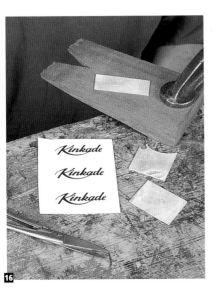

INLAYING A MOTHER-OF-PEARL LOGO

Mother-of-pearl is a delicate and fragile material; a design does not have to be complex to be effective. Think carefully and choose a logo design that is commensurate with your level of skill.

When you are happy with your design, make several photocopies of your artwork. Fasten one to the selected piece of mother-of-pearl with white (PVA) glue . When dry, cut carefully around the outline of the design using a jeweler's piercing saw and birdmouth support jig **17**. Practice is needed to exert the correct amount of pressure that will avoid excessive blade breakage. Use needle files to smooth any irregular edges. A complex logo may be cut in two sections to avoid snapping. When finished, remove the paper guide by soaking the piece in water to reveal the pearl shape **18**.

To create the relief in the headstock face, fasten another photocopy of the design in position with white glue. When dry, scribe around the outline with a sharp craft knife, scoring as deeply as possible into the veneer **19**. The hole is excavated using a miniature router, with a dental burr set to a depth slightly less than the thickness of the mother-of-pearl **20**. Using the photocopy as a guide, cut up to the scored line. Make the final fitting with small chisels and a knife, so that the inlay just drops into the hole without excess pressure, which might break it. Color some epoxy resin to match the wood by adding fine sawdust particles to the glue **21**. Use the colored epoxy to glue the logo in place. When set, sand the inlay and excess glue smooth with a sanding block, working progressively from coarse to fine grades **22**.

Neck Carving and Fingerboard Camber

- ■ **Planing the neck and fingerboard**
- ■ **Creating the camber**
- ■ **Final neck carving**
- ■ **Fingerboard inlaying**

Decisions on neck-depth, profile, and degree of camber across the surface of the fingerboard are very much matters of personal choice. The dimensions used in this book should suit most players, but some may want to alter one or more of them to suit an individual preference. Some shapes are more suitable for certain styles of playing—a "V" profile, for example,

suits players who bring their thumb around the back of the neck for fretting. You might decide to examine the dimensions and profile of a favorite instrument, and incorporate these into your design.

PLANING THE NECK AND FINGERBOARD

The neck has been left to settle for a couple of days, and you should now be able to see whether it has moved out of line. Protecting the soundboard with a clear acrylic sheet as a caul, plane the surface of the fingerboard straight **1**, reducing its depth to no less than ¼ in (6.5mm). A straight-edge held on the

surface of the fingerboard projecting over the body should reveal a gap at the bridge position of ⅜ in (9.5mm) **2**. You may need to plane more material from one end of the fingerboard than the other to achieve the correct height: this is the fine tuning of the neck-to-body pitch initiated earlier.

Plane the section of the fingerboard that sits on the body so that it slopes by about ³⁄₆₄ in (1mm) toward the soundhole **3**. This prevents the appearance of a "kick-up" as the neck pulls forward under the tension of the strings, and compensates in advance for any swelling of the soundboard during periods of high humidity.

CREATING THE CAMBER

Although you can, if you wish, leave the fingerboard dead flat, most acoustic guitars have a cambered fingerboard surface for ease of playing. The degree of camber is measured as the radius of a circle that would produce an arc that matches the curve across the surface of the fingerboard. I personally find that a compound camber, where the arc varies along the length of the fingerboard, gives the most comfortable playing action. The camber on my guitar is 12 in (300mm) at first fret position, and 14 in (350mm) at twelfth fret position.

To create the camber, carefully plane material from the edges of the fingerboard on both sides, working toward the middle **4**, and referring frequently to a radius gauge **5**. Use a straight-edge to ensure that you keep the neck true along its length. Smooth away any planing marks with a sanding block, working from coarse to fine grades **6**. Avoid rounding off the edges of the fingerboard, as they need to be sharp for accurate fret seating.

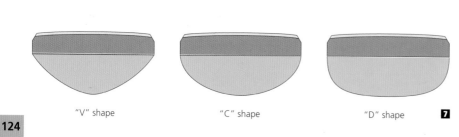

"V" shape   "C" shape   "D" shape   **7**

8

9

10

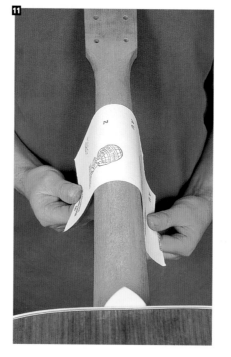

11

FINAL NECK CARVING

Diagram **7** shows the three most common neck profiles: select from a "V," "C," or "D" shape in cross-section. Reduce the neck to its final depth dimension and profile using a rasp, followed by a sanding block with 60 grit sandpaper **8**. This avoids creating hollows in the surface.

For the "C"-profile neck on the guitar made here, the finished depth at the first fret is $^{53}/_{64}$ in (21mm), and at the ninth fret $^{29}/_{32}$ in (23mm) **9**. Make an appropriately sized straight-edge to check for evenness along the neck surface **10**. Final smoothing can be done with a sheet of sandpaper drawn back and forth over the back of the neck as if you were polishing shoes **11**.

2

13

14

FINGERBOARD INLAYING

This can be as elaborate or as simple an affair as you care to make it. I have chosen to inlay this guitar with a subtle yet elegant set of squares and diamonds made from abalone shell. If you don't want to cut your own, many pre-cut shapes and designs are available from luthier suppliers.

Apply masking tape to the fingerboard, and accurately position the inlay with a dab of superglue, scribing around it with a sharp craft knife **12**. Remove the inlay and excavate its housing using a miniature router with a dental burr, in the same manner as the headstock inlay (see page 121). Clean up the corners with a small chisel **13**. Glue the inlay in position with colored epoxy **14**, and sand smooth with a sanding block, progressively reducing to 400 grade wet-and-dry paper **15**.

15

Kinkade Tip

The simplest form of inlay to fit is mother-of-pearl dots, which are widely available in a range of grades and colors. The hole is created using a brad-point drill bit in a drill press. Do a few tests on offcuts of fingerboard material to check that you can control the depth of cut.

Building the Guitar

Fretting

- ■ **Preparing slots and frets**
- ■ **Installing the frets**
- ■ **Fret dressing**
- ■ **Side dots and edge detail**

Fret wire comes in many sizes, all with different widths, crown heights, tang dimensions, and degrees of hardness. The choice of fret size is a matter of personal preference—different fret sizes suit different playing styles—although 99 per cent of acoustic guitars come fretted with medium-size wire. The hard-wearing wire that I use has a crown width of 0.080 in (2.03mm) and a crown height of 0.043 in (1.09mm). It arrives in my workshop in a 30-foot (10m) coil with an 8 in (200mm) radius.

▼ **Cross-section of fret wire in slot**

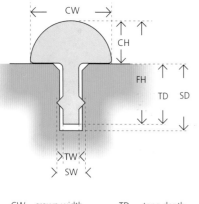

CW	crown width	TD	tang depth
CH	crown height	SW	stud width
FH	fret wire height	SD	slot depth
TW	tang width		

▼ **Comparison of fret wire sizes**

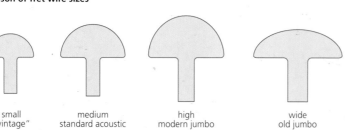

| small "vintage" | medium standard acoustic | high modern jumbo | wide old jumbo |

The guitar's fretboard is the principal point of contact for the player and has a huge influence not only on how the instrument plays, but on how it is perceived. A good guitar can be ruined by a bad fretting job. Conversely, a poorer-quality instrument can be made to play well with a slick fret-dressing and set-up.

PREPARING SLOTS AND FRETS

Any fretting job is only as good as the seating of the fret. For best results the slot must be prepared meticulously to fit the chosen fret wire in every respect. Traditionally, fret wire is held in place by the wedging action of the tang studs in a slightly undersize slot (see diagram left). This must be judged with care,

however: if the frets are installed too tightly, the combined compression effect will cause a reverse bow in the neck.

Another way is to cut the slot to the full width of the stud and glue the frets in place with epoxy resin filling the gaps. This is believed to give better transference of energy from the fret wire to the fingerboard, and is worth bearing in mind should you have problems with other methods.

Here we use the traditional approach, with the added precaution of a dab of glue in the slot to hold the frets in place should the fingerboard shrink and the slot-width increase.

Cutting the fret slots

Check the surface of the fingerboard for straightness and angle, and remedy

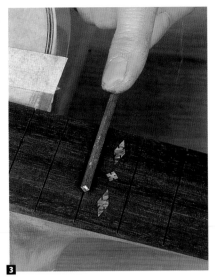

if necessary **1**. The fingerboard has been planed for camber since the initial fret slots were cut, and these must now be finessed for width and depth to suit our chosen fretwire. Take a fretsaw of the desired blade width and practice creating accurate slots on a fingerboard offcut. The required slot-width varies a little from wood to wood: rosewood, for example, allows a narrower slot-width than ebony for the same sized wire because, being softer, it has more give. For ebony I use a slot width of 0.0235 in (0.6mm). Carefully cut the slots to the correct width, and overdepth by 15 per cent **2**. Use a small square-section file to bevel the top edges of the slot **3**. This step helps the frets seat fully, since fret wire is made by extrusion and does not have crisp corners. It also reduces chipping during re-fretting procedures.

Preparing the fret wire

If your fret wire came in straight lengths, bend it into a curve slightly tighter than that of the fingerboard

using an appropriate tool. Use wire snippers to cut the wire into ¼ in (6.5mm) overlength pieces to match each fret position **4**. Emphasize the curve in the wire at each end with standard pliers: this helps with seating at the fret ends. Set the frets aside in the order that they will be fitted.

INSTALLING THE FRETS

Dribble some water into each fret slot followed by a dab of AR glue **5**, and wipe away the excess. Support the neck with one hand behind the fret position and place the fret over its slot. With a fretting hammer, tap down each end **6** before working toward the middle **7**.

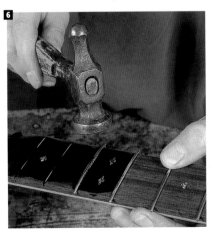

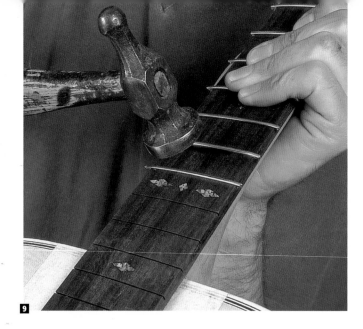

This action creates a bayonet fitting of the tangs at the fret ends: these are pushed sideways as the middle of the fret is seated, leaving the tang with no direct path to retrace, which reduces

the chances of a lifting fret. Wipe away glue squeeze-out with a damp cloth **8**. Check that the seating is perfect.

Continue to work your way along the fingerboard, cushioning the blows from

the hammer by supporting the neck from underneath **9** **10**. When you reach the last few frets over the body, absorb the energy from the hammer with a weighted caul held inside the guitar **11**. Alternatively, you can press them home using a caul and clamps **12**. A fret press is a useful tool for pushing the frets into position **13** once the ends have been tapped down. Unfortunately it can only be used from the first to the ninth frets, after which the heel obstructs its use.

Sight down the fingerboard to spot any badly seated frets **14**, and double-check with a straight-edge. Any rocking of the edge indicates a high fret. Leave overnight to dry and settle.

FRET DRESSING

Reattach the protective caul to the soundboard; then trim the fret ends using flush-cutting snips **15**. Take care not to unseat the frets or dent the soundboard as you work. File the fret ends smooth using a single-cut file **16**

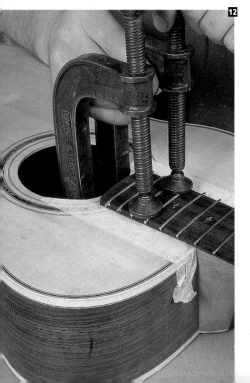

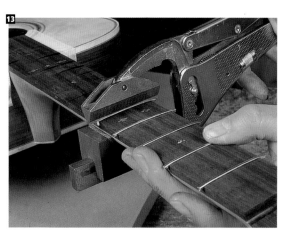

14

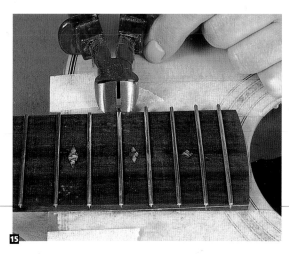

15

16

and bevel them to an angle of about 35 degrees **17**. Continue to file until you have beveled the edge of the fingerboard, creating a flat surface about ¹⁄₃₂ in (0.75mm) across. This ensures the guitar will be comfortable to play.

Leveling the fret tops

No matter how carefully you installed them, some of your frets are sure to be high. This next process levels their tops and should transform them into the smoothest frets you have ever played on. It must be done against a good light source, enabling you to see marks reflected on the surface of the frets.

Check the neck and, if necessary, adjust the trussrod for straightness. Wearing a protective face mask, and with the neck of the guitar supported, use the coarse face of a combination carborundum stone to grind the tops of the frets. Work up and down the length of the fingerboard, and then diagonally, until you have touched the surface of every fret **18**. Check for curves with a straight-edge. Turn the stone over to its fine face and grind out the scratches made by the coarse face, again working up and down the fingerboard. Your frets now have completely flat tops **19**. If you notice that some have a wider flat surface than others, don't panic: you'll deal with that next.

Recrowning

This process restores the half-round profile to the flattened fret tops after

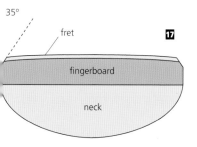

35°

fret

17

fingerboard

neck

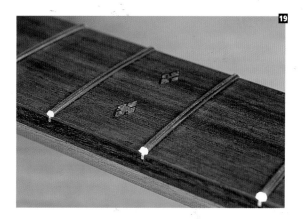

18

19

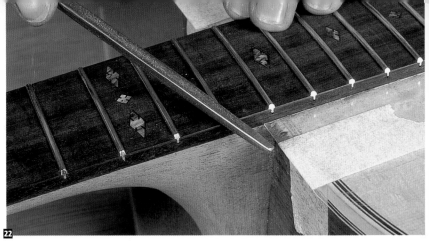

21

file

before crowning   after crowning

after

sharp corners   before

leveling. My favorite tool for this job is a triangular file whose edges I have ground smooth to prevent it marking the fingerboard surface, but other tools could be adapted equally well. Shape each side of the fret until there is only a narrow sliver of ground surface from

the carborundum stone showing along the length of the fret **20** **21**. Round off the sharp edges on the sides, and on the beveled faces of the fret ends **22**.

Using the fine carborundum stone, grind the tops of the frets across the fingerboard (that is, along their length).

Polishing the frets

The dressed and crowned frets are now polished to a high luster. First work up and down the fingerboard with 400-grade wet-and-dry paper, rounding over the tops of the frets and removing the marks left by the stone **23**. Then rub the paper along the length of the fret, across the fingerboard. Repeat this

▶ **Recrowning the frets**
*The fret on the left
has not yet been
recrowned, while the
fret on the right has.*

process working through the grades from 400, to 600, to 800, to 1000, finishing with 1200-grade paper. Always work along the fingerboard first and finish across the board, along the length of the fret 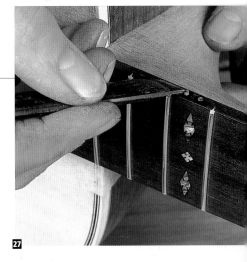. This ensures scratch-free frets for smooth string bending. Use worn-out 1200-grade wet-and-dry paper on a sanding block to finish off across the board **25**. Your frets should now have a glorious shine. Finish them off with 0000-grade wire wool—anything coarser will ruin your good work—using your fingernails to push the wool into the angle between fret and board.

SIDE DOTS AND EDGE DETAIL

Drill holes for the 1/16 in (2mm) abalone side dots using a miniature drill with an appropriate bit **26**. The dots are fixed in place with superglue **27**, then sanded flush to the surface.

The final job is to sand the neck edge of the fingerboard **28**, rounding it off into the profile of the back of the neck.

Kinkade Safety Tip

The dust from carborundum stone and wire wool is reported to be hazardous, and may be a carcinogen. Always wear a face mask throughout the leveling process.

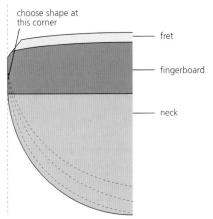

▼ **Profile of neck edge after sanding**

choose shape at this corner

fret

fingerboard

neck

Building the Guitar

Finishing

- ■ **Preparation**
- ■ **Oil finish**
- ■ **Waterborne lacquer**

The finish on a guitar is intended to enhance the natural beauty of the wood as well as to seal the surface against dirt. Depending on its type and thickness, the finish may also confer a degree of protection against damage, but there's a balance to be struck: too thick a finish can dramatically dampen the guitar's tonal response.

Over the centuries, various finishes have been used, from egg white, oil, and shellac, to cellulose, polyurethane, and polyester. Recently developed waterborne lacquers address important environmental issues by emitting fewer volatile organic compounds, or solvents, during the drying process.

Before you decide which finish to use, test one or two alternatives on offcuts of your construction materials. This gives the best possible sense of how the finish looks "on the wood."

PREPARATION

For all types of finish the first step is immaculate preparation. You've heard it a hundred times, but here it is again:

the finish can only ever be as good as the surface underneath. Thorough groundwork is critical and should not be skipped or skimped. Always wash your hands before you start, as oil from your fingers may inhibit bonding.

Filling gaps

Fill any small gaps at the fret ends, using superglue mixed with an appropriate colored wood dust. Fill any gaps around the bindings in a similar way. Sand smooth.

Sanding

Many people regard the sanding-down stage as a chore, but I'd encourage you to enjoy it. Up to now, making your guitar has involved you in an extremely complicated woodworking project. But as you begin to refine the surface of the instrument, a transformation takes place: a beautiful musical instrument is emerging before your eyes. All the care

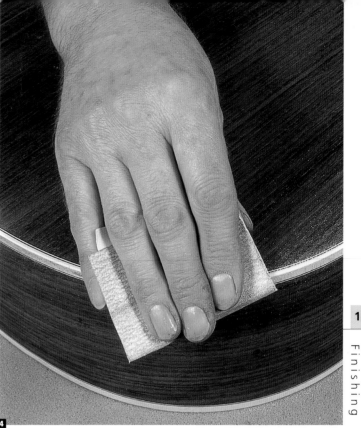

3 **4**

and attention you have invested in the building process has been worthwhile. Your guitar is "becoming real."

Always sand in the direction of the grain, and clean away dust particles from previous grades with a tack rag. Start by sanding the woods that create the darkest colors of dust, in this case the back, sides, and neck. Then clean the guitar and working area completely, and proceed to the soundboard. Sanding in this order ensures you finish with a clean spruce soundboard.

Do the initial sanding with a palm sander, loaded with 150-grit silicon carbide paper **1**. Proceed on flat surfaces with scrapers **2** and sanding blocks **3**. On curved surfaces use a folded sheet of sandpaper **4**. Work through the grades from 150, 180, 220, 320, and continue with 400-grit wet-and-dry carborundum paper **5**. For waterborne finishes, a dampening of the wood surface during the initial sanding processes is necessary. This raises the grain, which is then flattened back when dry with the next grade of paper. For oil finishes, continue to sand with grades 600, 800, and 1000 of wet-and-dry paper.

5

Kinkade Tip

Wet-and-dry carborundum paper can be used either wet or dry, as its name suggests. In these sanding processes it is used dry. Use it wet with soapy water when cutting back coats of lacquer.

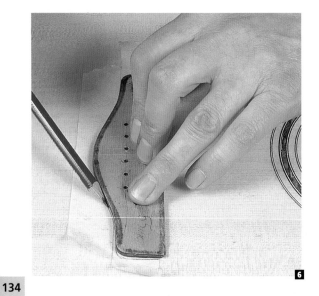

6

7

8

9

Masking

The areas of the guitar that do not require any finish are now masked for protection. Locate and mark the position of the front edge of the bridge by measuring 25¼ in (641mm) down the centerline of the fingerboard from the nut position. Using a template of the bridge shape, mask an area ³⁄₃₂ in (2mm) smaller than the bridge **6**. Mask the soundhole to stop the finish soiling the inside of the guitar **7**. Mask the fingerboard **8** and the nut seating trench **9**. Make a hook from a wire coat hanger and suspend it from the ceiling in a well-lit area. Reflections from the light source enable you to see how much finish you are applying. All finishing must be done in a dust-free environment with a temperature of around 65°F (18°C) and low humidity.

OIL FINISH

First experiment with different brands of oil on offcuts to observe the various levels of sheen that can be achieved.

Clean the guitar with a tack rag. If the manufacturer makes a sealing product to complement their oil, use it as a first coat. Apply the oil sparingly, wiping it on in the direction of the grain with a small pad made from an old cotton T-shirt. Holding the guitar by the neck, begin on the soundboard **10**, then proceed to the back, sides, and headstock. Hang the guitar on the hanger suspended from the ceiling, and complete the process at the neck **11**. Leave to dry overnight.

Lightly sand the guitar with 1200-grit wet-and-dry paper. Clean the surfaces with a tack rag and apply a coat of oil with a fresh cotton pad, as sparingly and evenly as possible. This process requires practice—too much oil will create runs that must be mopped up immediately. When you are satisfied with the result, leave to dry overnight. On oily woods like rosewood the oil may not dry completely, so apply a sealing coat of dilute shellac.

Repeat this sanding and re-oiling process eight to twelve times until the desired level of finish is achieved. Leave for a few days to harden. The final sanding is done with either well-used 1200-grit wet-and-dry paper, or micro-mesh paper, grade 3000 upward, using light pressure and sanding in the direction of the grain **12**. Buff up the surface using a soft cloth. To achieve a satin effect, rub gently with 0000-grade wire wool, then buff with a soft cloth.

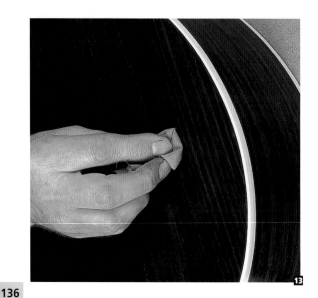

13

14

WATERBORNE LACQUER

In all lacquering processes the material is applied coat-on-coat until it is thick enough to be sanded optically flat. The surface is then polished to a high gloss, taking care not to rub through to the wood underneath. Some practice is required to gain an understanding of the rate at which the lacquer coat builds up. You also need to avoid applying too much lacquer, since this has a detrimental effect on the tone of the instrument.

Seal the guitar with waterborne lacquer diluted 50/50 with water. Apply with a pad made from an old cotton T-shirt **13**. Grain-fill open-pored woods—such as rosewood, mahogany, and walnut—with an appropriately colored filler, taking care to keep the filler well away from the soundboard. An old credit card makes a good spatula for this job **14**! Wipe away the excess and leave to dry overnight. Sand back to the wood surface **15**. Wipe off the dust with a tack rag, reseal, leave to dry, and sand lightly.

Most lacquers can be applied by brush, so there is no need to invest in expensive spraying equipment. A spray gun is quicker and applies a more even coat, but is less economical in volume of lacquer used, due to the losses in overspray. You can apply waterborne lacquers with a sponge brush bought from your local hardware store, or other wide, soft-haired brushes available from artists' suppliers. Wipe off the dust with a tack rag and apply a reasonably thick coat of lacquer in strokes that overlap by ¼ in (6mm), working across the surface **16**. The lacquer appears somewhat milky at this stage, but becomes clear as it dries. If it appears very white you are applying too much.

15

16

Kinkade Tip

French polish is an alternative finish you might consider. It is environmentally friendly, inexpensive, and imparts a delightful sheen. It has excellent tonal qualities and durability. It is best learned from a practical demonstration, or you could find an instruction manual and experiment for yourself.

Apply the lacquer to the guitar in the same order as described on page 135. Leave to dry for a couple of hours, or as recommended by the manufacturer. Lightly sand the surface with 400-grit wet-and-dry paper **17**, and recoat.

Apply two to three coats of lacquer per day, with a more vigorous sanding after every third coat. Depending on the lacquer and the thickness of individual coats, between six and nine coats will be required altogether.

Alternatively, apply the lacquer with an appropriate spray gun, following the manufacturer's guidelines on nozzle sizes and air pressures **18**. Leave to harden and cure for one week, depending on the lacquer brand. Then use a sanding block to cut back the lacquer with 1200-grit wet-and-dry sandpaper that has been soaked in warm soapy water for 30 minutes, until all the surfaces are uniformly flat with no pores or dimples showing. Polish the surface with micro-mesh paper, working from grade 3200 to 4000, 6000, 8000, and 12,000. Complete the process with polishing cream, rubbing the surface to a high luster **19**.

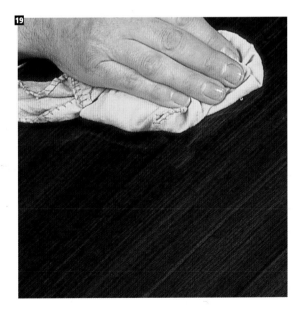

The Bridge and Scratch Plate

- **Making the bridge**
- **Fitting the bridge**
- **Preparing the scratch plate**

Earlier we stressed the importance of accuracy when cutting the fret slots. The same precision is required in the making and correct positioning of the bridge, which both anchors and determines the length of the strings.

MAKING THE BRIDGE

It is important that the bridge fits the soundboard perfectly before the two parts are glued together. I find it easier to achieve this perfect fit while the bridge is still an oversize rectangular blank measuring $6\frac{19}{32}$ x $1\frac{3}{4}$ x $\frac{7}{16}$ in (165 x 45 x 12mm). Even if you have constructed your guitar with a flat top, it is likely to have developed a slight dome by now. Alternatively, the surface may be slightly concave, as the result of lowering humidity levels. On no account try to glue a flat-bottomed bridge to the domed or concave top of a guitar; instead shape the gluing surface of the bridge blank with a scraper to fit the curvature of the soundboard **1**. Once a fit has been achieved, trace the outline of the

1

bridge shape to the underside of the blank **2** then cut outside the line on a band saw **3**. Trim the excess depth of the bridge wings on the band saw. Shape to the line, taking care not to chip the edge of the gluing surface **4**. Sculpt the top surface of the bridge. Remember that its overall height should be $\frac{1}{32}$–$\frac{3}{64}$ in (0.5–1mm) higher than the line of the top of the frets at the bridge position. Sand smooth, working down to 400-grit wet-and-dry sandpaper to achieve a polished finish **5**.

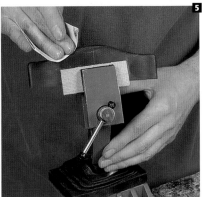

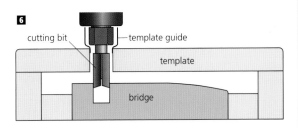

cutting bit — template guide

template

bridge

Kinkade Tip

It is possible to cut the saddle slot by hand using knives and small chisels, but the difficulty lies in leaving the bottom of the slot dead flat. Good contact between the saddle and the bottom of the slot is extremely important for the efficient transfer of the vibrating strings' energy through to the soundboard. Incorrect fitting will have a severely detrimental effect on the tone of the instrument.

Referring to the plans, set up a router with a ⅜ in (10mm) template guide and a straight ⅛ in (3mm) twin flute tungsten carbide cutting bit, and cut a ⅛ in (3mm) wide saddle slot to within ⅛ in (3mm) of the overall depth of the bridge, for example, a ¼ in (7mm) deep slot in a ⅜ in (10mm) deep bridge **6**. Use a jig to hold the bridge in place **7**. Note that the slot is angled: this is known as compensation, and is explained in greater detail in the next section.

Forming the pinholes

Mark out the bridge pinhole positions.
Remember these holes determine the
string position at the bridge so accuracy
is paramount. Drill the holes using a
³⁄₁₆ in (4.5mm) brad-point drill bit that
will not drift off line **8**. Bevel the top
edge with a countersink bit. Finally,
ream out the holes to fit the taper of
the bridge pins **9**.

FITTING THE BRIDGE

This is one of the most important
stages in building the guitar: if the
bridge is not accurately positioned, the
instrument will not play in tune.

Locating the bridge

Carefully remove the masking tape
from the soundhole, fingerboard,
and bridge position. Tape the bridge
lightly in its approximate location
25¼ in (641mm) from the nut position,
aligned centrally to the fingerboard.
Check the sideways alignment of the
bridge by holding a piece of fine cord
10 to mimic the line of the two outside
strings, ⅛ in (3.2mm) in from the edge
of the fingerboard to the center of the
bridge pinholes, and adjust as necessary
by moving the bridge from side to side.

The other dimension to check is the
distance from the nut to the front edge
of the saddle slot. The first string—top
E—is compensated by adding ⁵⁄₆₄ in
(2mm) to the scale length, and the sixth
string—bottom E—by adding ¹⁵⁄₆₄ in
(6mm). Technically speaking, the level

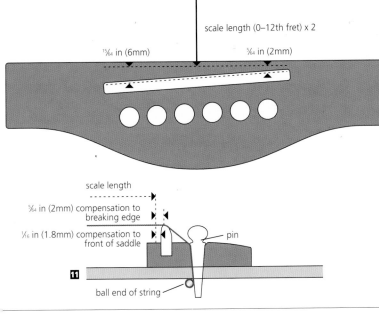

scale length (0–12th fret) x 2

$^{15}\!/_{64}$ in (6mm)

$^{5}\!/_{64}$ in (2mm)

scale length

$^{5}\!/_{64}$ in (2mm) compensation to breaking edge

$^{1}\!/_{16}$ in (1.8mm) compensation to front of saddle

pin

11

ball end of string

12

of compensation required varies with different string gauges and action heights. Unlike an electric guitar, however, with its individual string saddles adjustable for height and length, an acoustic guitar simply doesn't have a facility for fine-tuning, so these dimensions give the best compromise. Bearing in mind that the saddle will have a slightly rounded profile to ease the path of the string resting on it, the compensation at the front edge of the saddle slot at the first string position should be $^{1}\!/_{16}$ in (1.8mm) **11**. To allow for any shrinkage in the fingerboard during construction we now reset the bridge position so that the distance from the nut to the front edge of the saddle at the first string position equals double the distance from the nut to the center of the twelfth fret plus $^{1}\!/_{16}$ in (1.8mm) **12**.

Gluing the bridge

Double-check these measurements, then hold the bridge steady with masking tape, and clamp firmly with a caul inside the instrument. Drill through the two outside bridge pinholes—first and sixth—with a $^{3}\!/_{16}$ in (4.5mm) bit **13**. Two bridge pins covered with adhesive tape as a glue barrier will serve as locating pins during the gluing process.

Scrape back the lacquer on the soundboard under the bridge position,

13

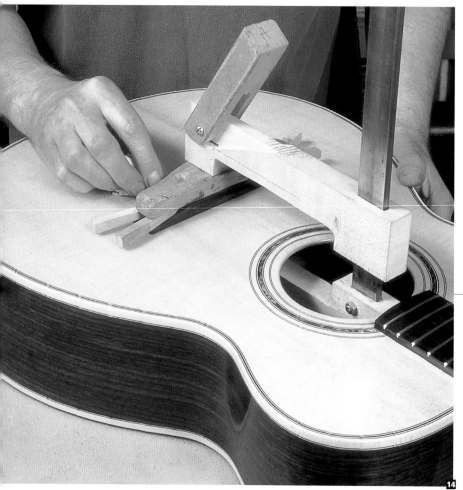

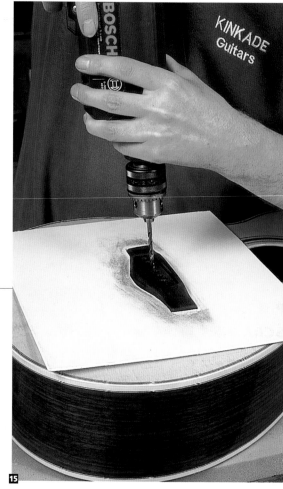

to within $\frac{1}{32}$ in (1mm) of the inside edge of the bridge, ensuring a neat lacquer-to-bridge detail. Make a caul the same shape as the bridge, with two holes to accommodate the pin positions. Apply AR glue to the bottom of the bridge and the soundboard, and clamp the bridge in place **14**. Wedges at the ends of the caul help to keep the edges of the bridge firmly seated. Clean away glue squeeze-out with damp tissues, and take care to avoid denting the surface of the soundboard, especially on an oil finish. Leave to dry overnight.

Unclamp and drill the remaining pinholes **15**, protecting the soundboard with a cardboard caul. Use a reamer to finesse the fit of the bridge pins **16**.

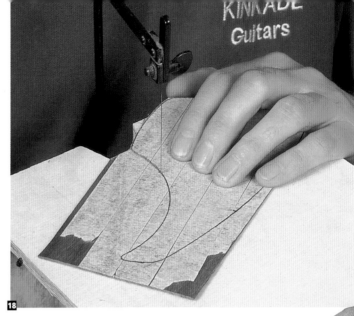

PREPARING THE SCRATCH PLATE

You may feel, having spent so much time building a wooden instrument, that the addition of a plastic scratch plate seems inappropriate. You may even decide not to fit one at all, since many fingerpickers never mark the soundboard. But on an oil-finished instrument a scratch plate does offer some necessary protection, and I favor making one from wood.

Prepare a slice of suitable wood—here I have chosen quarter-sawn walnut—to a uniform $\frac{1}{16}$ in (1.5mm) thickness. Use a transparent template of the scratch plate to help you orientate the grain direction. Apply masking tape to the underside of the scratch plate wood and trace the outline **17**. Using a piercing saw, cut outside the line, from the underside to avoid chipout **18**. Sand carefully back to the line—wood as thin as this is very fragile. Bevel the edges and sand to a smooth finish with fine grades of paper **19**. Check the fit, especially its alignment with the rosette **20**.

The scratch plate is fitted in position after setting up the guitar, as described in the next chapter.

Setting Up

- **Fitting the tuning machines**
- **Fitting the nut**
- **Making the saddle**
- **Cutting nut slots**
- **Neck relief**
- **Final set-up**
- **End-pin label and scratch plate**

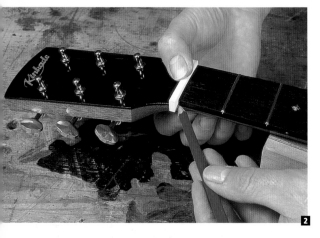

Your project is coming to fruition, and you are fast approaching the moment you have been dreaming about. A word of caution: do not rush the final stages in your eagerness to coax the first sounds from your instrument. As ever, care and accuracy are required when making and fitting these last crucial parts. They have a direct effect upon how well your guitar will play and sound.

FITTING THE TUNING MACHINES

Clean up any lacquer that may have found its way into the tuning machine holes. Ensuring that your holes are the right size—the wedging action in too small a hole could cause the headstock to split—carefully press the bushings into place, using a padded caul to avoid damage to the finish **1**. Align the tuning machines, drill pilot holes for the fixing screws, and screw in place.

FITTING THE NUT

Clean up any finish from the nut trench. Check the seating of the bone nut blank prepared earlier (see page 120) **2**. Mark it for length and trim to size carefully as the bone can chip easily. Shape it until it is overheight by $\frac{7}{64}$ in (3mm) on the bass side and $\frac{5}{64}$ in (2mm) on the treble side **3**. Check the seating is a good fit **4**. Glue in place with AR glue **5**; clean up any glue squeeze-out.

5   6

MAKING THE SADDLE

Sand an oversized bone saddle blank until it is a close fit in the saddle slot **6**. Sand its bottom surface flat and square to its sides **7**. Trim it to length **8**, rounding off its ends to match the slot shape. Bevel the edges of the bottom surfaces to ensure snag-free seating **9** and place in the slot **10**. The saddle should not wobble, yet be free enough to fall out when the guitar is turned upside-down.

7

8   9

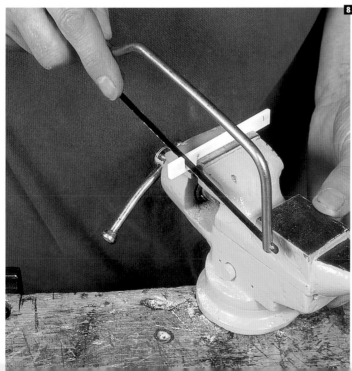

10

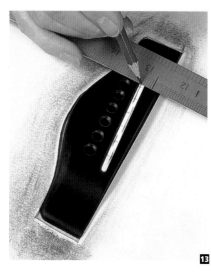

string needs more compensation than the top E string. The wound G string needs less, and so on. The top E string should be compensated by ⁵⁄₆₄ in (2mm) and the bottom E string by ¼ in (6.5mm) **13**. Shaping is carried out with small files. All surfaces should be gently rounded **14** and sanded smooth down to 1000-grit wet-and-dry paper, to ease the path of the string, reducing string fatigue and subsequent breakage.

You can now use a straight edge to simulate the path of a string and estimate the curve of the top of the saddle **11**. File the saddle down carefully until the gap between the top of the twelfth fret and a straight edge resting on the first fret and the saddle top is ¹⁄₁₆ in (1.5mm) at the first string position and ⁵⁄₆₄ in (2mm) at the sixth string position. The camber of the saddle should make the action rise gradually from the first to the sixth string. Return the saddle to its slot **12**.

The top of the saddle can be shaped for more accurate intonation. The B

CUTTING NUT SLOTS

The slot cutting and string spacing at the nut is achieved with the help of the strings themselves. Strings set too close to the edge of a fingerboard are likely to be pulled off during playing. Fit the first and sixth strings (top and bottom E), loosely tensioned, with them resting on the surface of the nut. Position them ⅛ in (3mm) in from the edge of the fingerboard **15**. Control your excitement as you hear the first sounds coming out of your guitar. Mark the positions of the string centers on the nut with a 0.013 in (0.33mm) fret file

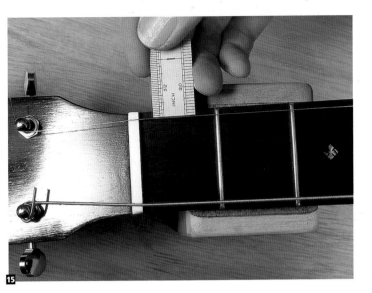

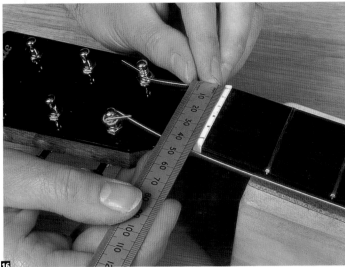

and divide the space between them for the four remaining strings . The strings can be equally spaced on their centers, or arranged so that the gaps between them are equal, or a hybrid approach may be taken.

Using suitable files, cut a slot for each string a little way into the nut 17. A file just wider than the string gauge will create a slot that facilitates easy passage of the string and frictionless tuning. If you make the slot too narrow, the string will snag and create tuning problems; make it too wide and the string will "drift" in the nut. Fit the remaining strings and assess the spacing at the nut 18. Spacing can be adjusted as the slots are cut deeper by moving them sideways a little. Do not cut the slots to their final depth just yet.

NECK RELIEF

Bring the strings up to tension to check the relief in the fingerboard. We do this by using the strings as a straight edge. Hold down the first string at first and fourteenth fret. Observe the gap

Kinkade Tip

People talk about a "straight neck" as if it was a wholly desirable thing. The truth is that the best guitar necks are not quite straight, but have a slight concave curve. In order to achieve the lowest, buzz-free playing action, the line of the frets should match the envelope of the vibrating string, which yields a curved line. The sixth string usually vibrates more freely than the first string, requiring more space and a higher action.

between the top of the sixth fret and the underside of the string 19. It should be between 0.005 and 0.015 in (0.1 and 0.35mm). The relief may be reduced if necessary by adjusting the trussrod. Insert an Allen key in the nut and turn clockwise: one-sixth of a turn should have quite an effect once the trussrod nut is tight to its bearing washer. OK, you can have a quick play to check the relief. Now back to setting up to improve playability.

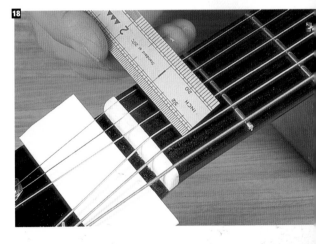

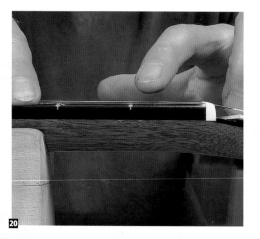
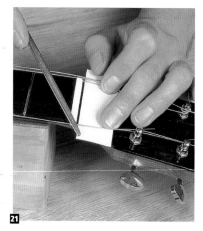
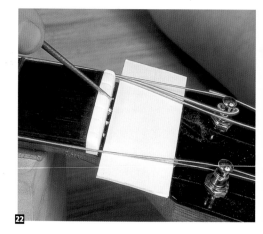

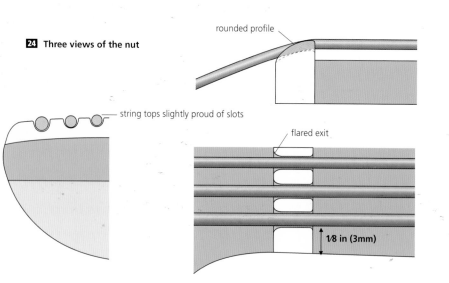

FINAL SET-UP

Return to the nut to finalize the depth of the slots. Hold each string down between the second and third frets, observing the gap between the top of the first fret and the underside of the string **20**. You need to reduce this gap to around 0.004 in (0.1mm). The fatter strings like more height than the thin ones. Beware of cutting the slots too low: the gap will disappear and the string height at the nut will be lower than the fret height, making the open strings buzz. Reduce the excess height of the nut with a file and round off all the sharp edges **21**. Flare out the exit path of the strings from the nut **22** and polish the slots down to 1000 grit wet-and-dry sandpaper. This will ensure a smooth passage of the strings **23 24**.

Check the action height of the guitar **25**. The gap from the top of the twelfth fret to the underside of the strings should be 5/64 in (2mm) at the first string and 7/64 in (2.5mm) at the sixth string for a medium action **26**. This height can be adjusted by removing material from the saddle to lower the action, or placing shims under the saddle to raise the action.

24 Three views of the nut

rounded profile

string tops slightly proud of slots

flared exit

1/8 in (3mm)

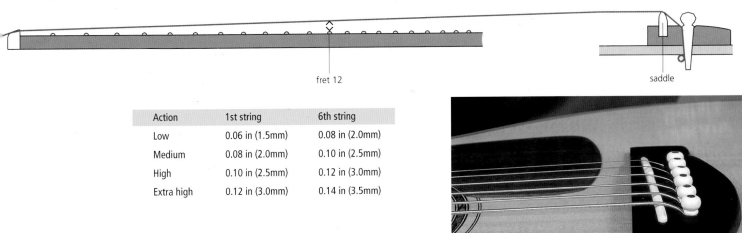

fret 12

saddle

Action	1st string	6th string
Low	0.06 in (1.5mm)	0.08 in (2.0mm)
Medium	0.08 in (2.0mm)	0.10 in (2.5mm)
High	0.10 in (2.5mm)	0.12 in (3.0mm)
Extra high	0.12 in (3.0mm)	0.14 in (3.5mm)

27

END PIN LABEL AND SCRATCH PLATE

Use a craft knife or needle file to notch a rounded path for the strings as they approach the bridge pinholes. The strings should pass over the saddle at a reasonable angle to create efficient tone transfer from the string to the soundboard **27**.

An end pin can be fitted by drilling a hole with a brad-point drill bit and opening it up with a reamer to match the taper of the end pin, which is a push fit **28**.

Fit a label in your guitar with a name, number, date, signature, and any other information you wish to convey **29**.

Remove the masking tape from the underside of the scratch plate, replacing it with double-sided adhesive tape. Position it carefully **30**, rubbing it down to fasten it. Finish it with a wipe of lemon oil.

JOURNEY'S END

The moment has arrived. Your labors are at an end, and the fine musical instrument you hold in your hands is its own reward.

Tune up your guitar and play a few choice chords. Appreciate the fabulous tone, knowing that it will mature with age, and that you will enjoy listening to it develop for as long as you have the guitar in your possession. Reflect on the fact that, whatever else you accomplish in your life, you have brought a thing of beauty into being, and that in itself is cause for celebration.

28

29

30

Care and Maintenance

■ **Strings**

■ **Cleaning**

■ **Tuning problems**

■ **Action problems**

■ **Storage**

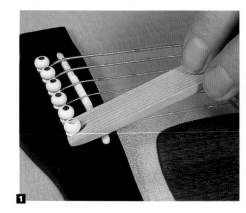

Your guitar is a robust instrument that demands little in the way of regular maintenance. Follow these simple steps to keep it in optimum condition:

STRINGS

Many factors affect the wear-rate of strings, from frequency of use to the pH value of the owner's perspiration, so there are no hard and fast rules about when to change them. Some players get three months from a set, while others are forced to change strings every couple of weeks. Be guided by sound and appearance: if the strings become dull, lose

their acoustic brightness, or are visibly clogged, it's time for a change. If one string breaks, then nine times out of ten it's best to change the set. Use only top quality brands, and experiment with different alloys—phosphor-bronze, bronze, or nickel—on the wound strings to see which suits you and your guitar. Manufacturers have recently introduced coated strings for extended life, which resist corrosion from sweat.

A simple puller made from a scrap of wood removes the bridge pins quickly and safely when changing strings, without resorting to pliers **1**. With the strings removed, rub the fingerboard with a few drops of lemon oil to

remove dirt and sweat deposits **2**. This keeps it in good condition and inhibits it from drying out and cracking.

When refitting strings, curling the end of the string ensures that the ball end sits against the bridge plate and does not snag on the end of the bridge pin **3**. Trap the tail of the string under itself to inhibit string slippage at the tuning machine **4**. A string winder makes a neat job of the windings **5**.

CLEANING

Buffing with a soft cloth is all that is necessary to clean the guitar, although numerous proprietory creams are available for guitars with a lacquered

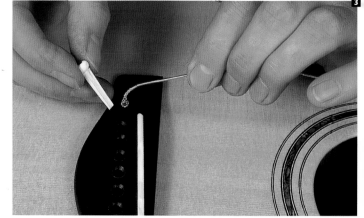

4

5

finish. Avoid using silicone wax-based products that might cause problems with a future refinish. An oil-finished guitar may be cleaned occasionally by wiping lemon oil over the whole instrument and then buffing it off.

TUNING PROBLEMS

If you experience problems with tuning stability and hear squeaking noises during tuning, the strings are probably sticking in the nut. Check the width of the slots and ensure that they are rounded and dressed downward from the fingerboard side. Polish with folded 1000 grit wet-and-dry sandpaper. Apply petroleum jelly or graphite dust scraped

from a 4B pencil to the slot  **6**. Check that the saddle is not worn or grooved, which can cause muffled tones and premature string breakage. If it is, round and polish the saddle smooth.

ACTION PROBLEMS

If, over a period of time, the action height rises, check for straightness by sighting down the neck from the headstock end or using the string as a straight edge. Remedy by turning the trussrod nut clockwise, which will pull the neck backward and reduce the action. If after resetting the neck you still need to lower the action, material can be removed from the saddle. To

maintain a good string break angle, material can also be shaved from the bridge, but beware of reducing the depth of the bridge to less than ¼ in (6.5mm) to avoid structural problems.

STORAGE

Keeping your guitar in a hard case when not in use **7** is the best insurance policy against accidental damage. Avoid leaving it in the sun, or in the trunk of a car on a hot day, where the heat could soften the glue and distort the timbers. Avoid extremes of humidity, which could cause changes in the action, or at worst, distortions or cracks in the neck and body of your guitar.

6

7

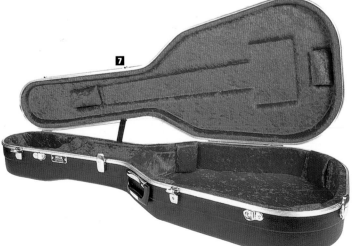

Amplification

- **Piezo bug**
- **"Under-the-saddle" piezo pick-up**
- **Magnetic pick-up**
- **Internal microphones**
- **Ibeam**

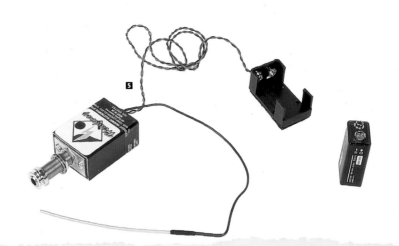

1

Building the Guitar

The quest for more volume—to enable the acoustic guitar player to perform on stage with louder instruments—has been a historic preoccupation of designer and makers. Milestones include the change from nylon to steel strings, the introduction of the arch-top guitar, and the invention of the resonator guitar. The pioneering use of electro-magnetic pick-ups in the 1930s led to the development of the solid body guitar, which could be louder than everything else put together. Magnetic pick-ups found their way onto production acoustic guitars in the late 1950s and early 1960s. They were also available as a retro-fit item clipped across the soundhole. And the introduction of piezo technology

marked a giant leap forward in the cause of amplifying the humble acoustic guitar.

Today many types of pick-up are to be had, and new designs appear all the time. Read the specialist magazines to keep up with developments, or consult your local supplier. Many players use several pick-ups on the same instrument, extracting the sonic qualities from each one and blending them together. Listed below are some currently available types. Acoustic pick-ups should be used in conjunction with a flat response amplifier such as a PA system or an acoustic guitar amplifier **1**.

3

PIEZO BUG

The first piezo pick-ups to be introduced were "bugs," which were simply attached to the soundboard with waxes or putties. These are still produced and are a low-budget choice. They can be used at low sound pressure

4

5

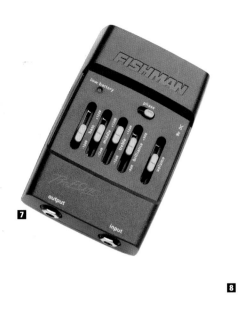

6

8

levels. They can sound somewhat boxy on their own, but are good for reproducing high frequencies in a blended system.

"UNDER-THE-SADDLE" PIEZO PICK-UP

This is the most common installation in factory-made guitars. It consists of a pressure-sensitive strip of piezo material **2**, **3** that sits at the bottom of the saddle slot **4**. It is important that the saddle is perfectly matched to the bottom of the slot for even downward pressure, and that it cannot wobble or tilt forward. Either will result in uneven string response when amplified. Different saddle materials can improve performance with some pick-ups. Man-

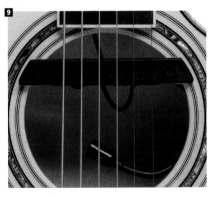

9

made products, such as micarta, have an even density, unlike natural bone. These pick-ups produce a low voltage output with an extremely high impedance. To capture their whole frequency output and response, they need pre-amplification and buffering from voltage leaking back from amplification systems. Manufacturers offer a choice of discreet onboard pre-amps without controls **5**, onboard pre-amps with controls **6**, or fully-featured outboard pre-amps to minimize the clutter of batteries and weight on the guitar **7**, **8**.

MAGNETIC PICK-UP

Magnetic pick-ups have improved vastly in recent years, due to the introduction of neodymium magnets, and inclusion of a pre-amp powered by miniature batteries fastened to the bottom of the pick-up. They are available in single coil and hum-canceling designs, and also with a mini-microphone on a gooseneck—internal or external—to blend with the magnetic sound. These are

becoming increasingly popular and sound excellent, although you can sometimes detect a hint of magnetic pick-up signature **9**.

INTERNAL MICROPHONES

These are available from most manufacturers and are susceptible to feedback. They are often supplied with "under-the-saddle"-type pick-ups for blending in and adding an acoustic breathiness to the sound.

THE IBEAM

This recently introduced pick-up design is a lightweight unit that adheres to the bridge plate on the underside of the soundboard opposite the saddle position. It produces a faithful acoustic sound, akin to a microphone **10**.

10

Glossary

Action The height of the strings above the fretboard; the ease with which the guitar can be fretted or played as a result of this distance.

Bindings Edge inlays that seal, protect, and decorate the guitar's body, neck, or headstock, made from wood or plastic.

Blocks Joining pieces that connect the sides, top, and back of the guitar at the top and bottom of the body. The top block also accommodates the neck joint.

Bookmatched Consecutive slices of wood joined at their edges to produce a mirror-image grain pattern are said to be bookmatched.

Bouts The upper and lower convex portions of the sides' curves, separated by the waist.

Braces Struts or bars inside the body, adding strength and optimizing acoustic properties.

Bridge The hardwood block on the soundboard that anchors and spaces the strings, and determines string length.

Compensation The difference between the theoretical string length, or scale length, and the actual string length.

Fingerboard or fretboard The hardwood board glued to the top of the neck, extending over the body, into which frets are installed.

Headstock The part of the neck at the top of the fretboard in which the tuning machines are mounted.

Kerfings Flexible strips of wood that provide both strength and extra gluing surfaces where the soundboard and back join the sides.

Heel The flared and reinforced section at the end of the neck where it joins the body.

Neck The piece of wood that protrudes from the body and supports the fingerboard and tuning machines.

Nut The small block of bone or plastic at the far end of the fingerboard over which the strings run to the tuning machines.

Pickguard or scratchplate A thin plate attached to the soundboard that offers protection from gouging plectrums and fingernails.

Purflings Decorative inlay strips, made of fiber, wood, or other materials used as edgings around the soundhole and along the edges next to the bindings.

Rosette The inlay around the soundhole, originally designed to protect the edge, but today purely decorative, often made from purflings and/or shell inlay.

Saddle The piece of bone or plastic that sits in a slot in the bridge and acts as a fulcrum for the strings at the body end. The saddle is often compensated for intonation.

Scale length The theoretical string length; double the distance from the nut to the center of the 12th fret.

Sides Curved pieces of wood that support the soundboard and back and give the guitar body its distinctive shape.

Soundhole The aperture cut in the soundboard, usually but not always rounded in shape, to allow amplified soundwaves to escape from the body, or resonating chamber, of the guitar.

Soundboard The face of the guitar where the soundhole and bridge are located; the primary sound-generating component of the guitar. Also known as the front, top, or table.

Tonewood Wood offering tonal qualities desirable in the making of instruments.

Trussrod A metal or graphite rod embedded in the neck that can be tensioned to counteract the pull of the strings.

Tuning machines The string winding mechanism fitted to the headstock.

Volute A lip carved in the back of the neck as it flares out to the headstock.

Waist The narrow portion of the body of the guitar between the upper and lower bouts.

Index

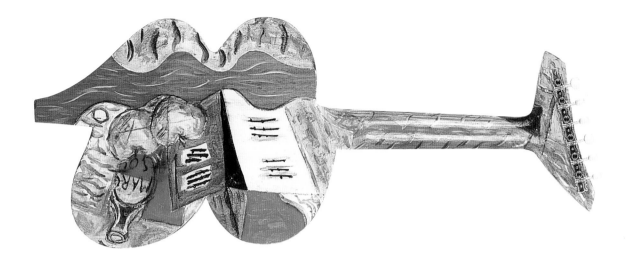

Credits

ACKNOWLEDGEMENTS

Writing this book proved a mammoth task and would not have been possible without my co-writer, who also happens to be my wife and life-companion, Carol Campbell. We worked together on the text for months in true partnership and some angst, and her commitment, insight, and writing skills were invaluable.

I also wish to acknowledge the support I've received from:

Piers Spence, my publisher and chief editor, whose love of guitars made this idea a reality; Kate Tuckett, Karla Jennings, Jill Mumford, and all of the dedicated staff at Quarto.

Patricia and Charles Aithie of Ffotograff, who survived the cramped conditions in my workshop and had to put up with my insatiable desire for the "best".

My customers, whose zeal (some call it an obsession!) for guitars, enchanting music-making and praise for my instruments make it all worthwhile.

Strings and Things Ltd for their support with Fishman Products.

FCN Music for their support with L.R.Baggs Products

My brother, Simon Kinkead, who was an integral part of Kinkade Guitars for the first 12 years and shared the passion.

The gifted luthier Les Luck, who inspired us both with his beautiful hand-made guitars and lit the beacon for us to see what was possible.

The following customers, who flocked to my door with their Kinkades when I needed examples of my design variations to be photographed for the book: Bob Slater, Damien Griffiths, David Kessler, Nigel Stacey, Noel Adams, Piers Spence, Richard Pendlebury, Roy Tucker, Steve Hart and Theresa Campbell.

Thank you one and all.

Jonathan Kinkead
Kinkade Guitars, 18 Clevedon Terrace, Kingsdown, Bristol BS6 5TX, United Kingdom
Telephone: +44(0)117 924 3279   Fax:+44(0)1275 817306
Website: **www.kinkadeguitars.co.uk**

SUPPLIERS

Allparts
PO Box 1318 Katy, TX 77492
Tel: (281) 391 7922
www.allparts.com

Guitar Parts USA
4833 Morning Drive, Amarillo, TX 79108
Tel: (806) 383 5148
www.guitarpartsusa.com

Luthiers Mercantile International Inc.
P O Box 774, 412 Moore Lane, Healdsburg
California 95448
Tel: (707) 433 1823
www.lmii.com

Martin Guitar Company
PO Box 329, 510 Sycamore Street, Nazareth, PA 18064
www.mguitar.com

Stewart-MacDonalds Guitar Shop Supply
Box 900, Athens, Ohio 45701
Tel: (800) 848 2273
www.stewmac.com

PICTURE CREDITS

p6, p7tr, Vintage Instruments, Inc. & Frederick W. Oster Fine Violins, Philadelphia, PA 215-545-1100, www.vintage-instruments.com
p8tl, Balafon Image Bank
p39bl, Nikon Corporation
p44, Paul Forester
p151 Hiscox Cases
p152t Marshall
p152 (no.2), p153tl, p153tc, p153bl, FCN Music/ www.fcnmusic.co.uk
p152 (no.3), p153tr, p153br, L R Baggs/www.lrbaggs.com
p152bl, p152br Headway Electronics
All other photographs and illustrations are the copyright of Quarto Publishing plc. While every effort has been made to credit contributors, Quarto would like to apologise should there have been any omissions or errors and undertakes to correct such in future editions.